PRAISE FOR *ASPIRE HIGHER*

"In *Aspire Higher*, Ken Lindner brings his complete and genuine depth of being to the reader in search of a successful and meaningful life. Ken writes out of his deep faith that each of us can become so much more than we may have imagined or believed. He has given us the gift of a book that acts both as a wonderful companion, as well as a guide, on a journey to deeper meaning and authenticity. Inspired by Ken's own personal life experience, his extraordinarily successful career, and his passionate love and faith in all of life's infinite possibilities, he teaches us to overcome our perceived limitations, reaching both inward and upward to become better and thereby make the world better as well. His book is important . . . and it is beautiful."

—Rabbi Eli Herscher, spiritual leader and teacher

"Helpful. Hopeful. Healing. *Aspire Higher* is a timely 'fresh word.' In a world of divisions, polarizations, scisms and isms—that should be wasms!—Ken Lindner navigates a path beyond positive thinking to positive living: psychological but not academic; spiritual but not religious; powerful and practical but not preachy. Most significantly this is a journey not 'to' your best self, but 'through' yourself as a life changing influence and impact on the lives of others. Do not write this work off as just another self-help product. This is a progressive pathway of love—not the mushy, shallow narcissistic type but one that equips you to touch and change the lives of those you love, and empowers you to love those you are yet to love."

—Kenneth C. Ulmer, DMin, PhD, senior pastor/teacher,
Faithful Central Bible Church

"This book emits so much light! It's good for the heart and soul, providing a step-by-step guide to more personal fulfillment and social harmony. An empowering and thought-provoking read. Thank you, Ken, for sharing your insights and wisdom."

—Ana Cabrera, host of *CNN Newsroom with Ana Cabrera*

"In his brilliantly crafted book *Aspire Higher*, Ken Lindner shows you step-by-step how to dramatically change your life for the better by changing your perspective, developing empowering self-love, and discovering your highest purpose. This is not just another self-help book filled with cliches and platitudes. This is a revolutionary guide that teaches you how to completely reframe the way you see yourself and others. The brilliance is in the sheer simplicity of the lessons. Inspiring and transformative, once you start reading this book, you realize how much it is truly needed right now in these chaotic and often difficult times. Ultimately, Lindner shows the reader how much broader your reach can be—how each of us can have a profound and positive effect on the world around us."

—Melanie Lawson, anchor, host, reporter,
KTRK-TV, ABC13 News

"This insightful and empowering book is the *ultimate roadmap* to elevating your life, your career, and your personal well-being. It equips you with proven skills to strategically navigate direct paths to enduring success, inner happiness, unconditional love for yourself and others, and deep fulfillment, even if you face major roadblocks along the way. Want to reach your fullest potential? 'Aspire Higher!'"

—Betty Nguyen, anchor, host, reporter, WPIX

"*Aspire Higher* is informational, inspirational, aspirational. Ken Lindner's new book paves the way for lasting inner fulfillment and peace, and peace among all people. What a true gift it is for all of us!"

—Shari Freis, longtime executive assistant to Ken Lindner

"Ken Lindner is a very thoughtful and introspective man. In these pages he gives us tools to ask ourselves probing questions. He hopes to impact the way we look at the world, clarify our goals, attain deep fulfillment, and achieve greater happiness. If you aspire to such a life, this book will be a great gift."

—Rabbi David Woznica, Stephen Wise Temple

"These challenging times present the perfect opportunity to reflect, reassess, and re-boot. In *Aspire Higher*, Ken Lindner provides an inspirational and relatable roadmap to help you live a purposeful and peace-filled life. Ken is a wonderful storyteller and a masterful strategist (in addition to being a gifted poet). The combination is a delightful read with brilliant lessons to savor, from a man who truly knows his stuff and is eager to share it with you. I am now reading *Aspire Higher* for the second time and have already dog-eared several pages!"

—Hosea Sanders, anchor, host, reporter, WLS-TV, ABC7 News

"With so much change and uncertainty in our lives, many feel a sense of being lost at sea. *Aspire Higher* provides a safe harbor, a tangible, positive, spiritual, and inspiring place to hold on to as we travel through life's challenges and opportunities. *Aspire Higher*'s steps and strategies are the empowering forces that will unlock the inner strength within you!"

—Don Browne, former executive vice president of NBC News and president of Telemundo and Broadcasting & Cable Hall of Fame honoree/inductee

"Ken Lindner's new book, *Aspire Higher*, creates a new awareness as to how we constructively face and thrive in today's challenging and complex world. By reading this breakthrough book, educators, schools, teachers, and parents will be far better equipped to empower students to make positive life choices that can and will lead them to live far happier and more fulfilling and productive lives. The information and philosophies of this book should continually be integrated into school curricula. Following the steps in *Aspire Higher* is the only way we can rebuild our spirits and our communities, based upon positivity, knowledge, and passion through aspiring to live your highest life. Thank you, Ken Lindner, for writing *Aspire Higher* and giving us the path and light to lift ourselves and those around us!"

—Metuka Benjamin, national and international educator

"Ken Lindner's book *Aspire Higher* isn't just a hit . . . it's a #1 hit! It's hard to describe how cool a #1 hit it is. We are all faced with challenges. It's life. Ken has accomplished the unthinkable. He describes in detail—and with answers—a process for dealing with life and succeeding! While the thought of being positive is everywhere, sacred texts from centuries ago mention how easy it is to reflect and concentrate on the negative. Ken has approached the concept of the negativity bias in a direct and fresh manner and gives you the mechanisms to conquer it and bring positivity and purpose into your life. We are all searching, hoping, wanting to do better in our lives. Ken Lindner is leading us all to a more promising, rewarding, and beautiful life. I can completely and unreservedly recommend *Aspire Higher* to everyone. Yes, everyone! Thank you, Ken Lindner."

—**Michael Lloyd,** music producer and songwriter

"In *Aspire Higher*, Ken Lindner aspires higher himself, offering readers a clear, practical formula to lead a love-filled, purposeful life by developing and expressing a higher love for themselves and for others. *Aspire Higher* is a great and necessary read for everyone in this age of doubt and division."

—**Kristen Sze,** anchor, host, reporter, KGO-TV, ABC7 News

"Ken Lindner's *Aspire Higher* gently and systematically reinforces with bootstraps why you are worthy of love and a life well-lived. As my Career Choreographer in the TV news business for 28 years, Ken's clarity and positivity have served as my guide for a long and joyful ride. His latest book takes you on a path of identifying and seeking your dreams, and gets you out of your self-sabotaging ways, so you can actively and decisively lean into the light and shine!"

—**Dominique Sachse,** mom, broadcast journalist, author, YouTuber, influencer, encourager

"Fear paralysis is real. If you're afraid or uncertain about what's ahead of you (I've been there), *Aspire Higher* is your book! What I love in these pages is that Ken Lindner generously gives us specific steps to help each of us discover, unapologetically, what we really value . . . and how to confidently move toward our aspirations."

—**Christi Paul,** host of CNN's *New Day Weekend*

"I found *Aspire Higher* to be the perfect prescription of inspiration that led me from a low point in my life, experiencing negative events, to one of hope and accepting the support and love around me. The book's messages encouraged me to change the course of my life and move forward with positive thoughts and actions. *Aspire Higher* has helped me convert what has been the most negative period of my adult life into an opportunity to grow, learn and find meaning from Positive Life Choice Psychology. Positive life choice, by positive life choice, I am rebuilding my life! What a gift! I am on my second read of the book."

—**A grateful reader of *Aspire Higher***

"Our society and world are filled with so much noise, misinformation, and division. It is vital that we return to truth, empathy, and humanity. In order to do so we must really know who we are as individuals and begin the work of living our most fulfilled and unified lives. *Aspire Higher* lays out the blueprint to do so in a way that will resonate with everyone from all walks of life. A must-read for those who want more for themselves and their neighbors."

—**Kelvin Washington,** anchor, host, correspondent, Spectrum News 1

"*Aspire Higher* and Positive Life Choice Psychology provide you with a path to inner peace and happiness that can radiate to everyone around you. Engage with this book as a favor to yourself, your neighbor, and the world."

—**Madison Alworth,** broadcast journalist

"*Aspire Higher* is a blueprint to develop your life, giving you the processes and techniques to realize your dreams. Ken Lindner has written a gem of a book, filled with concrete actions you can use to guide yourself to achieve your goals. It is an affirmation of you, and I'm sure it is a book you will return to again and again. I highly recommend this book to you, so you can guide your own journey."

—Jose Rios, former television news executive

"*Aspire Higher* is your playbook to get the most from what you desire in life. Ken Lindner walks you through easy-to-use strategies to effectively deal with life's most daunting challenges and plan a course of action to reach your loftiest goals. This book shows you how to build self-confidence and the courage to elevate your standing in life and become a positive influence on people around you. I am honored to provide this endorsement of *Aspire Higher*."

—Anne Holt, former news anchor and host

"This book is amazing. I couldn't put it down! *Aspire Higher* is uplifting and exudes positivity! In a pandemic, it's tough to look past uncertain times, but Ken Lindner shows us how to make the best of detours in life. He opened up about his vulnerabilities growing up and how he channeled his energy for better outcomes. The book is moving on so many levels and truly inspiring for all of us to add purpose in life and make the best of it!"

—Sandhya Patel, meteorologist, KGO-TV, ABC7 News

How to Find the Love, Positivity, and Purpose
to Elevate Your Life and the World!

ASPIRE HIGHER™

Ken Lindner

Founder of **Positive Life Choice Psychology**™

GREENLEAF
BOOK GROUP PRESS

Published by Greenleaf Book Group Press
Austin, Texas
www.gbgpress.com

Distributed by Greenleaf Book Group

For ordering information or special discounts for bulk purchases, please contact Greenleaf Book Group at PO Box 91869, Austin, TX 78709, 512.891.6100.

Design and composition by Greenleaf Book Group
Cover design by Greenleaf Book Group

Publisher's Cataloging-in-Publication data is available.

Print ISBN: 978-1-62634-904-9

eBook ISBN: 978-1-62634-905-6

Part of the Tree Neutral® program, which offsets the number of trees consumed in the production and printing of this book by taking proactive steps, such as planting trees in direct proportion to the number of trees used: www.treeneutral.com

Tree Neutral

Printed in the United States of America on acid-free paper

21 22 23 24 25 26   10 9 8 7 6 5 4 3 2 1

First Edition

To my amazing wife, Melinda, and our two wonderful children, Mary and Tristan. To our parents, Betty and Jack Lindner and Mary and Ross Myers, and to my loving family and extended family members. To all my treasured friends, and to you, the reader.

Thank you all so much!

The powerful play goes on,
and you may contribute a verse.
What will that verse be?
"O Me! O Life!"

—Walt Whitman

What you are about to read in *Aspire Higher* is the most important material that I will ever write. It is my verse—the heart and soul of my life's work. I believe that if you take the time to actively read and absorb the thoughts and steps herein, they will make a positive difference in how you write the future beautiful and loving verses of your life's play.

CONTENTS

AUTHOR'S NOTE

It is when we face our toughest
challenges, that we make our
greatest strides.

—KL

The pandemic has wrought worldwide devastation. As a nation, we are barely hanging by a thread; the same can be said for our world. Fear, division, violence, vitriol, and pent-up anger, as well as frustration, anxiety, and depression are pervasive. Racial tensions and feelings of helplessness and hopelessness abound. So many young people are scared and demoralized regarding the troubled, poisoned world that they are inheriting and have to survive in. We all have experienced so much profound loss—loss of loved ones and dear friends; loss of jobs, income, security, homes, and self-esteem; loss of the life and freedom that we once had and now so long for; and loss of our hope, positivity, and optimism.

As someone who watches television news, indelibly etched in my mind are the deeply disturbing images of people dying of COVID-19 or attached to ventilators, suffering all alone in over-crowded hospitals; the reprehensible racist actions that led to the Black Lives Matter protests, along with the violence and looting that accompanied them; stores and homes boarded up to protect them from vandalism and robbery; the unbridled hatred of people storming our Capitol as our elected officials fled for their lives and our police and military combated the insurrection; scores of heavily armed National Guard troops keeping watch over the Capitol 24/7; all of the individuals camped out on America's streets depicting the severe, heartbreaking homeless crisis in our country; rampant, horrific mass shootings; and the ugly racism and violence aimed at Asian Americans, simply because they are Asian. The appalling cycle of crime and violence against one another sadly continues.

It has been said that hatred corrodes the container it's carried in.[1] Our country and our world are in serious need of love, repair, and healing. We and the world continue to corrode at a rapid pace . . . and up until now, there hasn't been a solution or a happy ending in sight.

All of these feelings of negativity, pessimism, and helplessness bring to mind the poignant insight expressed in the film *Jerry Maguire*: "Breakdown? Breakthrough!" As with any breakdown, it's time for a breakthrough. As we hope to move past COVID-19, it's the perfect time for a breakthrough. The question is, what will that breakthrough look like for you, for our country, and for our world? Will you just "keep on keepin' on" and go back to the "same old," or will you take this golden opportunity to truly lift your life, your spirits, and your aspirations to a higher level?

Think about it. Has there ever been a better time than now to reboot your life and mindset, "think fresh," and in the process, substantially improve the quality of your life, the lives of others, and our world? I respectfully suggest that this is the perfect time to seize the life that you crave, become your best self, and enjoy your best and highest life by aspiring to more. You can do all of these highly beneficial things by developing the kind of authentic, unconditional self-love and love for others that will propel and motivate you to make positive life choices and do great things for yourself and for your life. And you will want to do these things when you feel that you and your well-being truly deserve the sweet fruits of life choices well made.

There are things in life that you can't control, but you *can* control your choices, values, attitude, perceptions, actions, and who and what you choose to include in your life. These are concrete and real elements that determine whether you are living your best and highest life and impacting others in a quality way.

Positive Life Choice Psychology™, or "*PLCP*," which comprises the foundation of this book, is not some amorphous, squishy, feel-good philosophy. On the contrary, it has as its basis a set of clear, logical, and accomplishable steps and strategies that will equip, enable, and—in the true sense of the word—*empower* you ("E3") to make positive choices throughout your life. As I will explain throughout our journey together, these positive and constructive life choices will significantly lift the quality of your life, and in the process, raise your self-image and enable you to enjoy strong feelings of healthy and catalyzing self-love. Then you, in turn, will be motivated to truly want to understand, respect, and develop compassion for others. You will be able to love more authentically. These highly potent feelings of love are contagious and will motivate the people around you to help and support others, thereby creating a country, and ideally a world, imbued with empathy, civility, peace, harmony, and respect for all individuals, regardless of their backgrounds, race, or gender.

Years ago, the Beatles shared the beautiful insight of "All You Need Is Love," and John Lennon asked us all to "Give Peace a Chance." As you explore the principles of *Positive Life Choice Psychology*, I ask that you give true self-love and inner peace a chance, as they are powerful feelings that can produce truly magical results!

You may have heard the concept going around lately that "love, not time, heals all wounds." Scores of material on this topic can be found just by entering these words into an online search bar. I am encouraged to hear that this mindset is growing. The original adage that this new one references—"time heals all wounds"—means quite the opposite; that one is asking us to sweep our pain under the rug and soldier on, rather than relying on connections with others to work through our injuries and grief. *Positive Life Choice Psychology* encourages you to support those around you, and to allow that support in when you yourself need it.

If you want to feel nourishing and empowering love in your heart; if you want meaning and positive purpose in your life; if you want to feel truly great about the person you've become and the way your life has evolved; if you want to live in a world filled with love, respect, empathy, and civility for all; and if you want to make a highly positive difference with your life, *Positive Life Choice Psychology* will show you how to accomplish and enjoy all of these wonderful things.

Above all, *Positive Life Choice Psychology* is a compelling call and guide for you to lift your game, aspire higher, and be your very best self.

INTRODUCTION

*If you want to turn the tide, the
change starts with you and the
choices that you make.*

—KL

THE PROFOUND POWER AND
IMPACT OF YOUR LIFE CHOICES

I am someone who experienced a number of psychological and
emotional challenges as a youngster. As I will discuss, the deeply
embedded, dark and debilitating perception of myself as unlovable,
not worthy of love or approval, and simply not good enough led me
to continually make poor and self-sabotaging decisions. Only when
I began to feel the love, valuing, and approval of my dad did I begin
to feel much better about myself. Through a set of game-changing
processes that I will explain later in this book, I became motivated
to make positive life choices for myself and for my life. When I
observed firsthand and reaped the wonderful benefits of positive life
choices well-made and effectively put into action, I realized how
incredibly life-changing and life-enhancing making positive life
choices can be for everyone.

Ever since then, I have studied and preciously valued the ideals and results that positive life choices bring to the table. And while making positive life choices is essential for you to reach and enjoy your fullest potentials, as you will see, everything starts with developing healthy self-love and then moves forward in an evolutionary process to feeling and expressing authentic Altruistic Love. Love is the supreme catalyst and the means for us all to heal and thrive. With these experiences, thoughts, and insights in mind, I founded and developed *Positive Life Choice Psychology*.

Positive Life Choice Psychology offers a lifestyle focused on making positive, constructive, and highly beneficial life choices so that you put yourself in the best position to attain and enjoy your fullest potentials and live your dreams. The explicit goal of *PLCP* is to equip you with the steps and Philosophies to attain a heart and soul filled with the love that will motivate you to want to lift the quality of your life and that of others.

As a late-blooming youngster, many of the individuals I interacted with early on in my life were unable to see my potential. Fortunately, I had a mom, a high school sociology teacher, and a tennis coach who did. In large part because these special and insightful individuals believed in me and my abilities, I was propelled and inspired to achieve many of my life goals. As a direct result of this unconditional support, my mission and calling in life are to envision "what can be" in others and to help them choreograph the strategic steps and positive life choices that enable them to take their potentials and turn them into wonderfully rewarding and fulfilling realities. Throughout my thirty-eight years of career counseling, I have helped many thousands of individuals to make a plethora of highly constructive and self-actualizing life and career decisions.

I graduated from Harvard University magna cum laude, and from Cornell Law School. At Harvard, I wrote an honors thesis on the psychological dynamics of decision-making, and I have been a passionate student of the art of making highly positive decisions ever since. At Cornell Law School, I learned how to think in a clear and orderly fashion, so as to spot the issue or challenge at hand and thereafter craft a logical set of steps to secure my best solution or resolution. My law school education gave me the foundation to create the hugely success-evoking process of Career Choreography™, which I practice with my clients daily. Additionally, I have written six books on the topic of life-choice-making, which in different ways embody and are a major component of *The Positive Life Choice Psychology Lifestyle*™ and its principles.

But enough about my background. *The PLCP Lifestyle* is all about *you*, and giving you the strategies and clarity to lift your self-esteem, aspirations, and life as a whole. Putting you in the right mindset is key. You absolutely have the awesome power to change and improve your life, starting today and for every day thereafter.

The **main keys to your success** are for you to:

- Know what you aspire to have in your life.

- Master your emotions, impulses, and urges and make them work for you so that you consistently make constructive, cognitively clear decisions.

- When you're called upon to make cognitively clear, positive decisions—during what I call *Crunch Time!* moments—*own* those decisions when you make them.

- Act consistently with those decisions so that you secure your desired results.

- Act in a manner that makes you feel really good and even *great* about how you've conducted yourself. Because if you feel good about your actions, the accompanying feelings of mastery and high self-worth, as well as your enhanced self-image, will empower and propel you to make more positive decisions moving forward. You will feel that you are worth making more good decisions for and that you truly have the ability to lift your life through your positive choices.

- Make choices and act in ways that respect, honor, enhance, and lift others. The beautiful by-product of this loving process is that you will continually instill love in your heart, which will propel you to consistently make highly beneficial future life choices that not only lift the quality of your life, but also the lives of those around you. If everyone adopts these goals and aspirations, as the legendary Sam Cooke wrote and sang, what a wonderful world this will be!

I am a huge proponent of any religion, philosophy, spirituality, or belief system that inspires and positively motivates individuals to aspire higher—that is, to strive for and practice appropriate self-love, to have love and compassion for others, to take the highest path, and to want to be the very best person they're capable of being.

This book and *The Positive Life Choice Psychology Lifestyle* are meant to be a companion to any religious or spiritual beliefs and life philosophies that you may have. That said, no religious or spiritual beliefs are necessary to have this book positively change your life in the most fantastic and fulfilling ways. Please remember that the virtues of love, compassion, kindness, true understanding of and respect for others, and wanting something far better for your life, the lives of those you love, and the lives of others are universal and not limited to any one religion or belief system. *The Positive Life Choice Psychology Lifestyle* is inclusive, nonjudgmental, egalitarian, and welcoming to all. It is highly insightful and can see the great potentials in all of us, yet is blind to skin color, gender, and economic station. It is a highly constructive, emotionally intelligent, and wisdom-imbued way of viewing life, navigating its often-choppy waters, and thriving spiritually and emotionally.

Aspire Higher and *Positive Life Choice Psychology* are a melding of an abundance of new material with ideas and concepts that I have presented and discussed in prior books, as over time I have refined and improved them and my thinking. Additionally, haven't you been to a place, or seen a person or a film, where upon initial viewing you didn't observe all there was to see or take in and understand all of the nuances and ramifications that you were able to the second or third time around? My goal in writing this book is to present you, the reader, with a compilation of my highest thoughts and tried-and-true processes.

Like the chambers of the heart, *Aspire Higher* is divided into four parts:

Part 1 explains what your *"Heart-of-Hearts"* is. This part focuses on *The Positive Life Choice Psychology* art of filling and refilling your *Heart-of-Hearts* with empowering feelings of accomplishment, high self-esteem, self-worth, self-love, and love of others, and then demonstrates why this process will be so beneficial and life-changing for you. Part 1 will also explain how to fill and refill your *Heart-of-Hearts* so that you are organically led time after time to do great things for yourself, your life, and ultimately, for others. This process constitutes the most beneficial form of self-help and self-determinism.

Part 2 discusses how to master your emotions, impulses, and urges so that they work in harmony with your intellect and your *Heart-of-Hearts*, with the result being that you make cognitively clear, highly positive life choices that reflect your highest and most dearly held values. By accomplishing this on a consistent basis, you instill positive, enhancing, and empowering feelings of self-confidence and self-worth into your *Heart-of-Hearts*. These feelings inevitably motivate you to do great things for yourself, your loved ones, and others.

Part 3 is devoted to explaining why it is essential to take focused time to explore and identify your most important and highest values—your "gold"—and the person you most want to be—your "truth." If you know your gold and your truth, you are then better able to make life-enhancing choices that reflect and are consistent with that gold and truth. The effective implementation of this process fills your *Heart-of-Hearts* with the confidence that you can indeed effect positive change in your life though the excellent and wise choices that you make—choices based on your gold and truth.

Part 4 presents *The Positive Life Choice Psychology Lifestyle Philosophies, Aspirations, and Ideals* that can lift your spirits, nourish your soul, and propel you to want to aspire higher. Embracing and putting into action the strong and highly positive messages embodied in these *Philosophies* will fill your *Heart-of-Hearts* with invaluable feelings of self-love which, in turn, will catalyze you to treasure your well-being; to listen to, understand, respect, have compassion and empathy for others; and to love unconditionally. And if, like everyone else, you've experienced hurt, rejection, anger, rage, and other feelings that have in some or many instances hardened your *Heart-of-Hearts*, embracing and following *The PLCP Philosophies, Aspirations, and Ideals* over time will help to dissipate those embedded hard feelings lodged within you, much like warmth and rock salt melt ice. Through this highly salutary transformation process, you will fill your *Heart-of-Hearts* with positive, loving, highly constructive thoughts, *Philosophies*, and scripts for behavior, all of which will motivate and inspire you to do great and beneficial things for yourself, those you love, and those around you. As a result, negative thoughts and feelings will have no space to reside in your *Heart-of-Hearts*, and if they somehow sneak in, they will be pushed right back out, as your refill process will be working full time to ensure that your *Heart-of-Hearts* is fortified and operating on a steady, constructive course.

Part 4 also shares words and concepts of love, soul-nourishing-connection, and healing. Adopting the essence and spirit of these words and concepts will propel you to aspire higher. Like the *PLCP Philosophies*, they will fill your *Heart-of-Hearts* with feelings of self-love, as well as love, compassion, and empathy for others. I will give you specific ideas about how to take your love and compassion for others and turn them into world-changing realities, in big or small ways. In this final part, I provide examples of *PLCP* Altruistic Love—the highest pinnacle you can reach in this journey—and how you can with great purpose share it with and bestow it on others. Altruistic Love is the final and ultimate puzzle piece of aspiring higher. It is what gives your life its greatest, highest, and most fulfilling purpose.

Most everyone wants more love in our hearts and in the world. What positively separates *Aspire Higher* from all other books is that *Aspire Higher* gives you the clear, achievable, and actionable steps to find, develop, instill, and share that love. Essentially, this book provides you with the foundation and fundamental principles you need to create a more loving and love-filled country and world.

ARE YOU READY?

Before we start our journey together, let's discuss two basic concepts. The first is the all-important question of "Are you truly ready to improve and lift your life?" Your answer to this question may well indicate how effective you will be in implementing *The PLCP Lifestyle*. Experience has taught me that not all individuals are ready at the same time to embrace a particular concept or a certain way of thinking or acting. I know that as a late bloomer in many areas, I didn't become a willing academic student until my senior year of high school. But when I was ready to commit to giving my studies the attention that they warranted, it made all the difference in the world as to the intensity of my focus, passion, and commitment, and to my ultimate success.

Attaining success in connection with any endeavor requires appropriate discipline, self-control, and delayed gratification. If you're not intellectually or emotionally ready to be engaged in and dialed into *The PLCP Lifestyle* process, exercising the discipline necessary to attain maximum success will be far more difficult for you. Without the requisite discipline, all too often you will be tempted to take the easy, alluring path of settling for the immediate gratification, when it is far wiser and more beneficial to forego the immediate, easy choice and wait for a far richer and more rewarding payoff down the road. Put another way, if you are psychologically ready to embrace *The PLCP Lifestyle*, you will be far more likely to be all-in regarding being disciplined enough, cognitively clear enough, and passionate enough to take the sometimes more difficult path to make great life decisions for yourself. Please know that if you exercise discipline at the appropriate times, "the juice is almost always so worth the squeeze!"

The key here is for you to be intellectually, psychologically, and emotionally ready to consistently make positive and constructive life choices from today on. These enhancing and highly beneficial choices will jump-start the all-important transformation process of raising your feelings of accomplishment and mastery, self-esteem, self-worth, and self-love, as well as your self-image. As you will see, these supremely empowering and motivating feelings will organically inspire and lead you to want to raise the quality of your life, the lives of those you love, and the lives of others. All are beautiful results of being ready and committed to the process.

So please ask yourself: "Am I truly ready to actively and zestfully seize a lifestyle that will motivate, propel, and put me in the best position to enjoy my optimal and highest life?"

DO I HAVE THE DESIRE TO "THINK FRESH"?

The next, related question is: "Do I truly desire to 'think fresh' and develop a new, open, and objective mindset and approach to making the decisions and life choices that will substantially improve my life?"

As we will discuss in more detail later, we develop our behavioral scripts to give us control of and predictability in our lives, keep us safe, protect us, and the like. As a result, we often do and perceive things in the exact same way for years and possibly for a lifetime. We have become a nation seeking affirmation and confirmation, not enlightening and enhancing information—especially if the views expressed differ substantially from our own. Witness the various news media that have attained huge success and profits by catering to a specific-minded group of viewers, listeners, and readers, giving them exactly what they want to hear.

The PLCP Lifestyle asks that you keep a completely open mind to new and possibly better and improved ways of viewing and making life choices, and behaving. Through a willingness to be open, objective, and hungry to learn and improve, you will truly grow and evolve. This makes sense, right? Your goal and that of *The PLCP Lifestyle* is to aspire higher by lifting your game, ideals, and life. All this can be accomplished by allowing and encouraging yourself to have the courage to venture out of your comfort zone and committing yourself to "think fresh," learn, evaluate, and then choose the most beneficial course of action for you and for those whose lives you touch and your life choices impact.

It's cool to say that you aspire,
And that the values you adopt
will lift you higher,
But worthy goals aren't attained
without the internal fire,
Of the motivating emotions
of want and desire!

—KL

I have experienced, seen, and counseled that, if you aspire to achieve a goal, "You've got to really want it, and you have to be fully focused on attaining it." There's no question about it. If you lack either the desire or the focus, you will too easily be diverted into settling for more immediate and ultimately less satisfying substitutes.

"Desire" is a powerful word. It conjures up highly energized concepts such as passion, need, and want. As we will discuss later, when these highly potent emotional energies are channeled toward healthy and constructive ends, they can have a *huge* positive impact upon your goal-attaining efforts. These energies can initially have a catalyzing and galvanizing effect on you. Thereafter, they can empower you to sustain your efforts and focus as you face challenging problems, crises, distractions, and weak moments.

You cannot repress or be shy about what you want in order to hide your goals and true feelings from yourself or others, or use rationalizations as a means of emotional protection should you fall short of accomplishing your goals. To the contrary, you must clearly identify your goals and not be afraid to put yourself squarely on the line in your efforts to achieve them. For example, professional athletes put themselves on the line each time they take the field or the court for a game, match, or competition. In each one of these instances, they risk not succeeding or winning their encounter, but put themselves on the line they must if they want to secure sweet, highly rewarding victories. Or, as they say, "If you don't get up to bat, you'll never [have the chance to] get a hit." So, go for the gusto in life and leave it all out on the court in order to live your optimal life and be your best self!

As we will discuss, in your quest to identify and attain your goals, you must not only identify your values, but you must also tap deeply into your desire and passion for goal attainment. You will need all of the desire and focus that you can muster when incorporating the arts of being disciplined and delaying gratification into your behavioral repertoires.

Individuals who accomplish their goals and live their dreams know what they want, and they have the drive, focus, and confidence to go after them.

So, if you are ready to aspire higher and be the happy, fulfilled, thriving individual you would love to be, let's begin a deep and illuminating dive into *The Positive Life Choice Psychology Lifestyle*.

Part 1

Your *Heart-of-Hearts*

In Part 1, we will discuss the all-important *Positive Life Choice Psychology Lifestyle* process of filling and refilling your *Heart-of-Hearts* with love and positive feelings—which includes filling it with self-love, respect, and compassion for and love of others, and a sincere appreciation of and gratitude for your life, blessings, gifts, and potential.

Before we delve into your *Heart-of-Hearts*, let's discuss three important concepts: "The Negativity Bias," how and why we create and maintain our behavioral scripts for navigating everyday life, and how *The PLCP Lifestyle* views the term "self-love."

"THE NEGATIVITY BIAS"

I have often wondered why so many people can have three or four great things happen during the day and experience one bad or unfortunate event, and they will be brought down by and continually focus on that one negative event, or why we "feel stuck on" or obsess about perceived negative or unpleasant experiences, encounters, or setbacks we've had. I'm sure that you have seen and personally experienced this pernicious dynamic at work.

When my daughter, Mary, and my son, Tristan, took a high school course in positive psychology, they introduced me to the concept of "the negativity bias." Because I found their explanations of the negativity bias so interesting and highly insightful as to why individuals so often automatically default to the negative perception of events, I was excited to learn much more about it.

The negativity bias explains why, when we are exposed to both positive and negative stimuli, we are predisposed and/or hardwired to focus far more, or possibly exclusively, on the negative. This means that negative comments, events, thoughts, emotions, and the like will have far more effect and impact on us and our emotional and psychological state and thought processes than positive ones.

Kendra Cherry, for verywellmind.com, writes that the "negative bias is our tendency not only to register negative stimuli more readily [than positive or neutral ones] but also to dwell on these events. Also known as positive-negative asymmetry, *this negativity bias means that we feel the sting of a rebuke more powerfully than we feel the joy of praise* [emphasis added]."[1]

PositivePsychology.com writes that "As human beings we tend to be impacted much more by negative events than positive ones," and that "Among other things, it [the negativity bias] can explain why we often:

- Recall and think about insults more than compliments.

- Respond more emotionally and physically to stimuli that are averse.

- Dwell on unpleasant or traumatic events more than pleasant ones; and

- Focus our attention more quickly on negative rather than on positive information."[2]

Along with the concept of the negativity bias is that of "negativity contagion," in which, according to the research conducted by Rozin and Royzman, "[perceived] negative events may have *more penetration of contagiousness* [on us] *than positive events* [emphasis added]."[3] Essentially these negative events affect us more and are imbued in our hearts, minds, and psyches a great deal more deeply and lastingly than are positive events.

According to PositivePsychology.com, the negativity bias is believed to be "an adaptive evolutionary function. Thousands of years ago, our ancestors were exposed to immediate environmental threats that we no longer need to worry about—predators, for example—and being more attentive to the negative stimuli played a useful role in survival."[4] However, this hardwired proclivity is no longer as useful for us as it once was, and it can have profoundly devastating effects on our self-esteem, self-image, psychological state, decision-making, relationships, and emotional well-being.[5]

According to negativity bias studies, not only do negative events have a greater impact on our brains, but the effects of these events last longer than positive ones, which is why past traumas that we've suffered have such long-lasting effects.[6] As the impact of the negativity bias can significantly influence whether we have the requisite amount of self-love, and are happy, fulfilled, confident, optimistic, constructive, and motivated enough to aspire higher, we will discuss this dynamic throughout this book.

So, if we, as Jackie DeShannon sang, want to place more love in our hearts, and develop deep, lasting self-love, self-respect, gratitude, as well as respect and love for others, we must combat and effectively master the negativity bias that looms in all of us. *Aspire Higher* and *The Positive Life Choice Psychology Lifestyle* will show you how to accomplish this.

OUR PERSONAL SCRIPTS
OF BEHAVIOR

Let's now focus on the two primary places our behavioral scripts originate: our genes and our environmental adaptations.

In connection with genetics, I would like to share the following insight with you, which was formulated and written by my mother, Betty Lindner, for her documentary about my father, *There Goes My Heart: The Jack Lindner Story*: "Some or many of our feelings, thoughts, behaviors, inclinations, and scripts are encoded in our ancestors' DNA. We in turn inherit these traits through our genes." Below is an excerpt regarding this process from my mother's documentary:

> *Believe it or not, there is an incredibly important "open secret" that most of us pay little or no attention to. I'm referring to a series of essential facts that affect each and every life to a considerable degree.*
>
> *Metaphorically, life is like a special kind of "scripted dream." A dream in very high definition. Our individual dreams are initiated when we are*

conceived; when sperm fertilizes the egg; and when the very first cell divides. Wondrously, it is then— from the highly complicated processes of combining, deleting, and recombining of DNA, RNA, genes, proteins, and the necessary chemistry—that, depending in part upon which genes are activated and which genes remain dormant along the way, our initial "personal scripts" originate and continue to develop with each cell division.

It should be noted that the "positives" (e.g., a Mozart's musical gifts) along with the "negatives" (e.g., "the sins of the fathers" and no less those "of the mothers") are all incorporated into the genes of offspring during this process. However, it is only when specific genes are activated and expressed in the then current scripts of their children that the "gifts" and "sins" of the parents are actually visited upon their children, who then continue the process when they subsequently procreate.

Hence, our genes are "hand-me-downs" and "carry-overs" inherited from our early forbears and direct ancestors. Thus, we are never tabula rasa, as our scripts are never blank. We are, in a manner of speaking, "time travelers" and "transporters" of our personal histories [thoughts, feelings, behaviors, and scripts] from eons of yesterdays, to millions of nows, which were once millions of tomorrows.

Our scripts are also determined by what we learn and experience throughout our lives. Therefore, both heredity (our genetic endowment) and environment play major roles in our scripting.

I agree with my mother's astute belief that some of our scripts of behavior are inherited from our ancestors, as they are encoded in our DNA and have been passed on from generation to generation.

The second primary means by which we derive our scripts is through life experiences or learned behaviors that we develop in order to help us get through life. Ironically, these coping mechanisms that we develop in order to protect us from (further) emotional, psychological, and/or physical pain are often the same defensive scripts that can lead us to take our most destructive and self-sabotaging actions. We will discuss the concept of learned behaviors as a means of survival and adaptation in more depth later in our journey.

SELF-LOVE

T*he PCLP Lifestyle* concept of self-love isn't one imbued with ego, vanity, or self-absorption. On the contrary, self-love is an absolutely necessary component of and catalyst for you to respect, value, cherish, and appreciate your mental, emotional, and physical well-being, blessings, unique gifts, life choices, and future. When you have a healthy amount of self-love in your *Heart-of-Hearts*, you will want to make positive life choices for yourself, because you authentically feel that your life, your health, and your future are worth making positive life choices for, time after time. Self-love enables you to recognize that you have the power to aspire higher and that you want more for your life; it also fuels and catalyzes you to elevate the quality of your life.

Self-love motivates you to do great things for yourself, and it is also the linchpin in the chain that ultimately leads you to respect, have compassion for, support, and love others. As we will discuss in depth later, developing the requisite amount of self-love is the essential first step in that chain. The second step is to attain accurate knowledge of others, which leads you to understand where others "are coming from" and why they view and value things as they do. With understanding of others comes respect for them; once you have understanding and respect for others, you can develop authentic compassion and empathy, which leads you to live a life of unconditional Altruistic Love.

Your feelings of self-love will also allow you to significantly lessen the often-deleterious effects of your negativity bias, as this bias can in part lead you down the destructive and dangerous path of feeling less than and hopeless. The negativity bias can also catalyze you to make harmful and self-sabotaging life choices, because you don't adequately value yourself, your abilities to take constructive ownership of your life, and your future.

Needless to say, having the requisite amount of self-love is essential if you want to enjoy your best life, fulfill your greatest potentials, love fully, and be your best self. So, now let's discuss how we effectively and with great enthusiasm fill our *Heart-of-Hearts* with self-love.

FILLING YOUR
HEART-OF-HEARTS

With a solid understanding of the above core concepts under our belts, let's now focus on how you instill that all-important self-love into your *Heart-of-Hearts*. In order to accomplish this, let's go all the way back to the beginning.

We all have a profound need to be loved, valued, respected, and treasured, a need that we experience in the deepest recesses of our being. This need is two-pronged: Not only must we be loved, valued, respected, and treasured, but we must also *feel* loved, valued, respected, and treasured by our parents, caregivers, and important others. Since children aren't mind-readers, the love given to them must be communicated in ways they can experience, recognize, and understand, from the moment of birth (initially through touch, sound, and warmth) onward. So even if parents have the best of intentions, if they can't effectively communicate their love to their children in a way that their children can understand, their feelings are all for naught. As time goes on, children will subjectively interpret the stimuli that they take in (how parents and others act toward them) as a means of determining how these key individuals feel about them. Ultimately, this input will figure into how these children will perceive and feel about themselves.

Additionally, given that we are all hardwired with some amount of negativity bias, infants and toddlers may well have a proclivity for focusing on the negative more than the positive. In fact, "One study found that infants as young as three months old showed signs of the negativity bias when making social evaluations of others."[1] According to the theory of "negative bias contagion," events the child perceives as negative may tend to penetrate the child's *Heart-of-Hearts*, mind, and psyche more deeply and may be more long-lasting than those events they perceive as positive. Taking the concept of the negativity bias a bit further, the more negative a child's (or an adult's) frame of mind becomes, they will quite possibly even perceive some or many positive events in their lives as negative as well; think of this phenomenon as the negativity bias snowball effect.

I remember when I was a youngster, I knew a girl who was very pretty, but she never felt that way or truly recognized her gifts because her mother, whether out of jealousy, insecurity, or some other agenda, continually denigrated the girl's looks. So even when others complimented the young girl on how nice she looked, the girl never believed the compliments. In fact, she would often respond by dismissing the compliment, citing some nonexistent skin or weight flaw that she perceived herself to have. For me, this was a sad state of affairs to witness, as this girl never saw herself as she truly appeared to others. I attribute this girl's exceedingly low self-image to her mother's incessant criticism and to the snowball effect of the girl's negativity bias, which exponentially increased the potency, impact, and staying power of those destructive comments.

In the big picture of my development, I realize that whether or not I felt that my needs were met or how I perceived that I was treated or valued in a given situation determined my feelings about certain situations or individuals, and whether I made constructive or destructive choices regarding them and in general thereafter. As I will explain later in more detail, when I was a young boy, I incorrectly perceived that my father didn't love me, because he was always working and never at home with me like my mom was. This led me to develop strong and painful feelings of hurt, rejection, unlovability, and hopelessness deep within me; and every time I felt rejected by my dad, these highly potent negative feelings triggered me to overeat and, in particular, to eat an excess of fattening foods, which led me to become obese. This obviously was highly toxic and self-destructive decision-making on my part, caused directly by how little I perceived that my dad thought of and valued me.

THE VULNERABLE CHILD HEART

How children's needs are met and how children subjectively perceive they are regarded can have a major and lasting impact upon them; ultimately, these perceptions often determine what scripts they will adopt and act out during the course of their lives. This concept can most easily be explained through imagination and visualization.

First, create and visualize in your mind a highly simplified metaphorical version of a child's heart. In the depths of this metaphorical heart is a magical place. This is similar to the metaphorical and/or metaphysical concept of the seat of your soul or the core of your being and acts much like the mind as it functions and relates to the brain. I refer to this metaphorical, magical place as the *Heart-of-Hearts*.

Except for a small but strong metaphorical magnet within that represents the child's fundamental and primal needs, the *Heart-of-Hearts* appears relatively[2] empty at birth. The primary function of this magnet is to attract and draw in emotional stimuli from the outer world.

Now think back and try to remember and visualize what it was like to be an innocent child with a profound need for love and approval in order to flourish psychologically, while at the same time being open, trusting, and defenseless against rejection, hurt, and disappointment—all of this at the hands of parents and/or significant, impactful others whom you were dependent upon during your childhood years. The subsequent influence that these individuals had on you and your *Heart-of-Hearts* was most profound. It touched and impacted the very core of your being for better or worse, depending on how you perceived the experiences. In this regard, you must stay fully aware that, because all children and adults are exposed to different stimuli and have varying amounts of the negativity bias, they each perceive and process experiences in their own subjective ways.

FILLING THE *HEART-OF-HEARTS*

Next, imagine that your *Heart-of-Hearts* is magical because it has the power to process one form of energy into another—such as when the gases of hydrogen and oxygen are transformed into water, or when water is boiled and transformed into steam, or when water is frozen and transformed into ice.

When the *Heart-of-Hearts* draws in the positive and negative stimuli that it receives from the outside world, it magically transforms them from sensory perceptions into various good and bad feelings that in turn fill it up. Thereafter, if the amount of felt love, positive valuing, and respect in the *Heart-of-Hearts* is plentiful enough to exceed a specific threshold (the near-complete filling of the *Heart-of-Hearts*), then there is enough love, high self-esteem, and self-respect for these feelings to be transformed into other feelings: first, into self-love; then, into the love of others; and finally, into unconditional love, or, as *The PLCP Lifestyle* calls it, Altruistic Love.

Feelings of being loved (lead to) → feelings of high self-esteem and self-respect → feelings of self-love → love of others → Altruistic Love.

Optimally, a child's *Heart-of-Hearts* will be filled to overflowing with feelings of love and being cherished, feelings that have been bestowed upon the child from the moment of birth by parents and/ or other key individuals. Once a child's *Heart-of-Hearts* is filled with love and other positive feelings, there will be little or no room left within it for any negative stimuli—including the negativity bias—to penetrate. In essence, the child's *Heart-of-Hearts* is so well insulated and fortified psychologically, emotionally, and spiritually by positive feelings that the negativity rolls off the child like water off a duck's back. Maybe this, in part, explains why some children and adults can be exposed to negative stimuli—such as violent films, TV programs, and music—without being affected by them, whereas others are catalyzed to commit destructive acts.

However, if a child's *Heart-of-Hearts* is left partially or totally unfilled with loving and positive feelings from parents and significant others, this emptiness can allow the magnet within (the child's needs) to indiscriminately attract both negative and positive stimuli that will fill the *Heart-of-Hearts*, with the big problem today being that there are so many negative stimuli in our society to attract. Hatred, rancor, divisiveness, distrust, violence, crime, racism, gender discrimination and misogyny, degrading music, and poor role models, to name just a few, are all intrusive forces waiting to prey upon a non-love-filled

Heart-of-Hearts. Additionally, when a *Heart-of-Hearts* isn't filled enough with fortifying feelings of self-love and high self-worth, the child can easily fall prey to their negativity bias.

In many instances, when feelings of being loved, valued, and respected aren't initially forthcoming from parents or key others in a child's life, and when the child perceives these positive feelings to be unavailable, I have learned from personal experience that the *Heart-of-Hearts* frequently fills up and begins to overflow with overwhelming feelings of hopelessness, unlovability, unworthiness, rejection, betrayal, inadequacy, shame, hurt, resentment, alienation, insecurity, and powerlessness, depending upon what the child perceives and/or experiences.

Along with the feelings of unlovability and hurt, the child also develops a sense of extreme vulnerability and an intense fear of having that vulnerability exposed. At some point during the process, the child's hunger for love, value, approval, and respect is psychologically suppressed. As a defense mechanism, the need is pressed back into the *Heart-of-Hearts*, where it is transformed. From then on, new needs arise, and behavioral scripts are developed to give the child perceived protection, power, control, and revenge. However, despite the fact that the child, teen, or adult develops and puts into place a large variety of rationalizations, as well as a number of other coping strategies and defense mechanisms (scripts), when frustration after frustration and hurt after hurt are added to the already existing negative feelings and negativity bias, they are all too often transformed—in the *Heart-of-Hearts*—into the unreasoning and powerful emotions of intense anger, rage, and hate.

Feeling unloved (leads to) → feelings of frustration → hopelessness → pain and hurt → resentment, anger, and rage → destructive and self-sabotaging behavior.

When these potentially toxic emotions come into play, as they inevitably will in many love- and respect-starved cases, those experiencing them can and often do develop damaging scripts and perpetrate destructive actions. These actions may be taken against oneself—like self-sabotage—or against others through deplorable acts such as (mass) shootings and destruction of others' property. Sometimes these actions aren't related to the behavior or the targeted person, such as in the instance of displaced anger when, for example, an employer has a negative encounter with his wife, child, or valued client and then yells at or humiliates someone else, such as an employee who played no role in the causal event, or when an enraged individual unleashes their intense anger by shooting random, innocent people.

I have also seen instances where the emotions of anger, hate, and rage can be totally out of proportion to the situations in which they were evoked. This might explain the extreme incident that I heard about when one student accidentally bumped into another student in the corridor of their high school. The student who was bumped reacted instantly by reaching into his backpack, pulling out a 9mm handgun, and shooting the student who bumped into him. Essentially, the seething anger within this person was like a keg of dynamite just looking and longing for a match and a flame. A more common example of this dynamic at work is when hurt after hurt and feelings of being disrespected and not valued continue to mount in one party in a personal relationship, and the aggrieved party holds it all in but is ready to explode at any moment. Then a relatively minor incident occurs that triggers an out-of-proportion vitriolic spewing or worse. Once again, this is a totally out-of-proportion response to the incident that triggered it.

When parents or key others don't fill their children's *Heart-of-Hearts* with enough love, and when their children fail to develop a strong sense of support, approval, and belonging, these children will find other ways to satisfy their needs; often the satisfaction of these intense needs results in individuals making destructive and self-sabotaging choices.

As I discussed above, early on in my life, I mistakenly believed my dad didn't love me, because he was always at work. I intuited that I must not be worthy of loving, which led me to develop and harbor deep feelings of rejection, hurt, and unlovability in my *Heart-of-Hearts*, which at some point transformed into feelings of anger and rage. These toxic feelings, in turn, led me to make negative choices, such as throwing a brick at my dad when I was four years old and acting out in other destructive ways as a means to get my dad to pay attention to me.

Only when I finally understood that my father worked six days a week and many evenings on top of that so my mother could stay home with me, and my parents could afford to give me a top-notch education, did I realize that my dad was away from our home, working hard so that I could enjoy the life he never had. When I began to bond with my dad through athletics and spend quality time with him, I also saw and felt that my dad loved spending time with me. I realized that my dad did in fact truly and deeply love me. And, when my mom explained that my dad's father, whom my dad loved very much, passed away when he was only four years old so that my dad didn't have a paternal role to emulate, I understood why my father had a hard time effectively communicating and interacting with me when I was young. All of these insights led me to develop feelings of love, respect, and understanding for my dad in my *Heart-of-Hearts*, replacing and transforming all of the negative feelings that were once deeply embedded in my *Heart-of-Hearts*.

During my late teens, I met two wonderful families, the Hartleys and the Bermans, who treated me like a treasured member of their beautiful families. They cared about me and gave their love and time to me unconditionally. Their sweet love poured into my *Heart-of-Hearts* and once again helped to further transform the negative feelings within me into loving and positive ones— like ice transforms into water when subjected to warmth.

After years of experiencing unconditional love from my parents, as well as from the Hartleys and the Bermans, my *Heart-of-Hearts* became full with love and positive feelings. This in turn led me to make positive life choices, such as being disciplined regarding my eating, which led me to lose a great deal of weight and to this day remain thin, and to channel my positive energies into highly constructive endeavors such as my athletics, schoolwork, work, and passion projects. All of these went well and instilled more and more positive, loving feelings in my *Heart-of-Hearts*. And at some point, when feelings of accomplishment and high self-esteem filled my *Heart-of Hearts* to a certain level, I organically began to care about and wanted to lift and enhance others and to be of service to them. Or, put another way, a good portion of the love that I received and that is embedded in my *Heart-of-Hearts* was trans-formed into a compassion for others and a strong, organic desire to pay that love forward to others.

I pray each day that I can live a life of service to others. I have chosen to be in a profession where I see what "can be" in others and help them to choreograph the steps that enable and empower them to attain their fullest potentials. The reason why I have written this and other books to enable others to self-actualize and live their very best lives is because I want to share the love I feel with others.

Please know that this altruistic, unconditional feeling and giv-ing of love isn't calculated or premeditated; quite the contrary, it naturally flows or overflows from a *Heart-of-Hearts* that is now full and fortified with feelings of love, accomplishment, and high self-esteem. And as you do generous and kind things for others, you continue to fill your *Heart-of-Hearts* with more feelings of love, accomplishment, and high self-esteem. So, loving, positive actions beget more loving, positive actions on your part.

Put another way, acting in loving, respectful, and compassionate ways as well as making positive life choices are like making savings bank account deposits. Each positive act or choice results in a highly beneficial deposit being made into your *Heart-of Hearts*. At some point thereafter, each of these empowering deposits is transformed in your *Heart-of-Hearts* into an improved self-image. These feelings and perceptions in turn lead you to feel that you are truly worth valuing, which motivates and incentivizes you to make more positive choices in the future because you authentically feel that you, your future, and your well-being are worth it! So, this becomes a highly positive and self-nurturing chain and cycle.

The basic law of one's *Heart-of-Hearts* is: *What goes into your* Heart-of-Hearts *comes out in one form or another. When love, respect, treasuring, and feelings of high self-esteem, along with other positive perceptions of yourself, reach a certain threshold in your* Heart-of-Hearts, *healthy and constructive feelings, choices, and acts will result. On the other hand, when negative feelings and perceptions of yourself fill it, unhealthy, toxic, self-sabotaging, and destructive feelings, choices, and behavior will be the result.*

SELF-LOVE AND SELF-RESPECT

We have all been exposed to a unique combination of healthy and unhealthy, and positive and negative experiences and values, and our *Heart-of-Hearts* have been filled accordingly with varying amounts of both positive and negative feelings and perceptions. For many of us, that fortuitous combination dictates how high or low our feelings of self-worth are, and how much, if any, self-love we have; it also can determine if we are indeed capable of generating any real self-respect and self-love; whether we can truly feel compassion, empathy, and love for others; and whether our behavioral scripts will be constructive and positive, or destructive and self-sabotaging.

Our major takeaway from all of this is that, if you feel great about yourself, your values, and how you live your life, you will be organically led to do good things for and with your life. Therefore, you want to proactively, consciously, and continually fill your *Heart-of-Hearts* with empowering feelings of positivity, goodness, mastery, and self-worth, because if you feel great about yourself, you will feel that you have the power to take constructive ownership of your life and your life choices.

The better you feel about the person you are, the more you will develop empowering feelings of self-love and self-respect, which will in turn fill your *Heart-of-Hearts* so that you want to make the effort to understand and respect others, have compassion and empathy for others, and unconditionally elevate and love others. If your *Heart-of-Hearts* is full with feelings of love, you are far more likely to continue to aspire higher and practice authentic altruism, which for us means that you do things because they are right and good and not because you expect anything in return.

OUR CONSCIOUS, COLLECTIVE COMMITMENT TO ASPIRE HIGHER

Picture a world where we see everyone and everything through the eyes of love, where we make the conscious choice to put positive feelings into our *Heart-of-Hearts*, as well as positive people, events, and values into our lives. Imagine a network of communities where people are committed to filling their *Heart-of-Hearts* with love, caring, understanding, and respect for everyone. This will equip, enable, and truly empower (E3) our society and our world like never before to rise to its greatest heights, because we in unison are authentically working together, hand-in-hand, *Heart-of-Hearts* to *Heart-of-Hearts*, with a mission and a social contract based upon respect, understanding, love, compassion, true caring, and empathy.

In order to accomplish this lofty set of goals, you must consciously and with great care fill—or refill—your *Heart-of-Hearts* with positive feelings, self-nurturing, high ideals and aspirations, and empowering experiences and acts. By filling our *Heart-of-Hearts* with love—for ourselves and all others—we win individually, because we feel *great* about ourselves, our potentials, our futures, and the individuals whom we have evolved into. Our society will also win, *collectively*, because we will all be living in a world of harmony, peace, and love, having as its roots the supreme values of love, understanding, respect, compassion, civility, and the strong desire to aspire higher. This is our conscious, collective commitment to and contract with each other to find positivity and purpose in our lives and to elevate our country and our world!

YOUR CHILD'S *HEART-OF-HEARTS*— A PARENT'S PROFOUND RESPONSIBILITY

From the day of birth, with no exceptions
Instill self-worth—so that your child's perceptions,
Are that they're valued in every way.
Make sure you take the time to say,
That you truly love them—so that they know it.
Being there for them is a way to show it.
Just keep on giving, with no measuring,

Your focused attention, and love-filled treasuring.
And if all of these qualities are instilled,
Their Heart-of-Hearts *will be filled.*
Then negative stimuli can't get in.
And destructive behavior won't begin.
If you lay a loving and respectful foundation,
Perceptions and feelings go through transformation.
Where SELF-LOVE becomes a love of others,
With the goal of enhancing their sisters and brothers.
And then your focus will go on to be
Raising the quality of our society.
But, if somehow you choose not to be there,
And if your child doesn't feel that you truly care,
Their Heart-of-Hearts *will become a place,*
That's empty, and just the sort of space,
That will attract the kind of negativity,
That's polluting our society.
If parenting isn't lovingly performed,
Perceptions and feelings will be transformed.
And the intensity of the anger and the fear,
May well shift up another gear.
And one day soon, there is no doubt,
Violence will be acted out.
Their painful feelings, children will avenge—
Through destruction, they exact revenge.

So, remember:
Instilling love is where it starts,
Love must fill their Heart-of-Hearts.
Your child needs to be lovingly insulated,

Or parental responsibilities you will have abdicated.
As to whether your child emotionally sinks or soars,
DEPENDS ON YOU. THE CHOICE IS YOURS!

And now that you're older, you now know,
That if you truly want to thrive and grow
Having true self-love is where it starts,
With it you fill your Heart-of-Hearts.
And if you do, you have the ability,
To be the very best, that you can be!

—KL

Part 2

How to Make Cognitively Clear Choices That Reflect Your Highest Values and Highest Self

5

HOW YOUR EMOTIONS & IMPULSES CAN AFFECT YOUR LIFE CHOICES, SELF-ESTEEM, & SELF-IMAGE

An essential process of *The PLCP Lifestyle* is making cognitively clear and highest-value-driven choices that reflect your best self. With this in mind, let's discuss how your potentially toxic emotions, impulses, and urges can dismantle your ability to think clearly, effectively, and constructively when you make choices and decisions and thereafter act.

By way of example, I'd like to share an incident that profoundly touched me, which took place when I was fifteen years old. My good friend Steve and I were going to Madison Square Garden to watch a New York Knicks basketball game. Before the game, we went to one of my favorite restaurants, which served flame-grilled steaks and huge baked potatoes topped with lots of sour cream, butter, bacon, and other goodies. Also on the menu were scrumptious desserts and big soft drinks. A dinner fit for a king or queen!

As we arrived at the end of the serving line with our trays brimming with food, we saw that all of the tables on the first floor of the restaurant were filled. So, we decided to carefully walk up the stairs with our loaded trays to find seating on the second floor. As we arrived upstairs, all of the tables were occupied as well, but eagle-eye Steve immediately spotted a table that was about to be vacated. In a flash, Steve made a beeline for it, but when he was almost there, another young man collided with him, and all of Steve's and the young man's food and their humongous drinks spilled all over both of them. Steve was a sopping mess, as was the young man. All of the plates, plastic glasses, and silverware fell to the floor with a thud. Instantly, like a powder keg exploding, Steve, at the top of his lungs, yelled at the young man, "What are you, an *idiot*?" For what seemed like an eternity, the restaurant was deathly silent. When the proverbial dust settled and we all saw the young man nervously trying to find his walking stick that had fallen on the floor, we realized that the young man wasn't "an idiot"—he was blind.

A second or two later, a lady sitting nearby graciously picked up the young man's walking stick and handed it to him. For the next moment or two, the soaking-wet young man apologized profusely for the mishap and then slunk into the elevator, accompanied by the woman who had brought him to the restaurant.

Steve and I couldn't have felt worse. We were mortified!

Let's analyze this highly disturbing encounter:

- We have a stimulus—Steve and the young man unintentionally bump into each other while carrying trays full of food. The food and drinks spill all over them.

- Steve is immediately overcome with the emotions of anger and rage. He instantaneously and unthinkingly reacts with a violent verbal assault against the young man.

- Then, with the invaluable benefit of a moment's cooldown and a clear observation and analysis of the true situation, Steve's heart and psyche were flooded with feelings of shame, embarrassment, and regret. On the heels of these feelings, Steve recognized that he had messed up badly, and he sincerely acknowledged that, in hindsight, he should have acted with more understanding and compassion. In other words, his best path by far in this instance would have been to aspire higher, not get enveloped in the web of his hijacking emotions, cool down, and then accurately assess the situation and choose his wisest course of action.

No question, this was an emotional and cognitive breakdown, which led to a breakthrough. I believe to this day, both Steve and I carry with us and are guided by that breakthrough, which is: Do not let your best judgment and highest self be hijacked and enveloped in a vortex of emotions, such as anger, rage, hurt, shame, or feelings of disrespect, hopelessness, desperation, or betrayal, and then unthinkingly react in a destructive and/or self-sabotaging manner. Not only can this reactive behavior be extremely hurtful to others, but it sends negative feelings and messages into your *Heart-of-Hearts*. In Steve's case, he was ashamed by how he acted. This inner acknowledgment lowered his feelings of self-worth along with his self-image, and made him feel bad about himself.

Here's another story on this same subject.

As a youngster, I vividly remember watching a National Basketball Association playoff game one rainy Sunday afternoon. It was a pivotal game for the New York Knicks, who had a chance to become the NBA champions. It was late in the fourth quarter and the score was tied. Walt Frazier, the star guard who set the tempo for the Knicks, had already scored a slew of clutch baskets and was single-handedly keeping his team in the game. With a couple of minutes to go, Frazier scored again to put the Knicks in the lead. As the play went to the other side of the court, when no one was looking, one of the opposing players viciously rapped Frazier on the back of the head and brought him to his knees. However, Frazier didn't lose his composure or his concentration. Nor did he, in a fit of anger, try to retaliate in kind and thus risk being thrown out of that crucial game. Instead, he calmly picked himself up, kept his laser focus, ran right by the assailant, and a moment later scored the final and winning basket. The sweetest outcome of all!

Upon reflection, I believe that Frazier said to himself after he was hit: "What do I do? Do I go after the player who hit me and maybe get myself ejected from this crucial game? Or do I focus and win the series with and for my team?" I feel that Frazier insightfully and constructively *chose* his course of action based upon what he valued most—winning the NBA title with the Knicks.

I learned a great lesson that day: to appreciate the huge value of self-control, and to calmly, consciously, and thoughtfully choose my responses to stimuli, based upon my truest and most cherished values and goals. Soon thereafter, I composed the following reminder for myself:

No matter how intense the emotion
or how loud the noise,
I'll make sure that I think clearly
and never lose my poise.

So here we have two similar stories with very different outcomes and effects on the individuals' *Heart-of-Hearts*. In both cases, an event took place: Steve bumping into the blind young man and spilling his food and drink all over him, and Walt Frazier being hit viciously on the head by a player on the opposing team, in an effort to possibly injure Frazier, throw his concentration off, or have Frazier retaliate in kind and be ejected from the game. In Steve's case, he let his anger cloud his best judgment and he, without thinking and accurately evaluating the situation, acted badly. He hurt and embarrassed the young blind man and was self-sabotaging, as he significantly lowered his feelings of self-worth. On the other hand, Walt Frazier appeared to evaluate the situation clearly and decisively. Although he could have succumbed to his potentially toxic emotions, instead, he chose to ignore his assailant and focus on attaining his preeminent goal—winning an important playoff game. I would think that this kind of stellar choice-making raised Frazier's feelings of self-esteem, along with the confidence that he indeed had the power to lift the quality of his life and his own esteem through the choices he made.

THE IMPORTANCE OF MASTERING YOUR EMOTIONS AND IMPULSES

We let our emotions
take over our lives every day!
—COLIN COWHERD,
nationally syndicated radio host

As you may have gleaned from Steve's and Walt Frazier's stories, the ability to master your emotions and impulses is essential if you want to enjoy your best life and be your best self. This is the case for a number of reasons. Let's examine the basis for this assertion:

- We have already discussed the concept that if your *Heart-of-Hearts* is full with feelings of love, high self-esteem, and the like, you are far more likely to want to do good and great things for yourself and for others. If good, positive, and loving feelings and perceptions are instilled into your *Heart-of-Hearts*, positive and loving feelings, choices, and actions will be the result.

- If we make constructive, beneficial, and healthy decisions and choices for ourselves and/or others, we instill highly positive and empowering feelings of accomplishment and mastery in our *Heart-of-Hearts*. When we intellectually and emotionally process the idea that we can take positive ownership of our choices and life paths, we gain the motivation and confidence to continue to make great decisions. And making great decisions feels good, as such decisions provide concrete evidence that we can indeed positively impact and lift our lives; and because we have strong feelings of self-love embedded in our *Heart-of-Hearts*, we feel that we deserve the sweet fruits of choices well-conceived and well-made. As a direct result, we are inspired to act in highly beneficial ways both for ourselves and for others.

- Whereas our wise and beneficial choices lead us to make more and more positive choices, poor, destructive, and self-sabotaging decisions make us feel bad about ourselves and our ability to positively impact and lift our life. Essentially, we feel defeated, hopeless, and impotent to take ownership of our life. A vicious cycle of poor decision-making is the deleterious result, as we lose the confidence, motivation, and discipline necessary to make enhancing decisions. We continue down a destructive path and inevitably continue to make bad choices that reflect our negative feelings of low self-worth and hopelessness.

- Put succinctly, making positive and constructive choices leads to more positive and constructive choices. Conversely, poor, destructive, and self-sabotaging decision-making leads to more bad decisions. As we continue to feel worse about our lot in life and our inability to positively impact the future, our negativity bias kicks in, which can incrementally or exponentially ramp up our feelings of hopelessness—we then become headed for a pernicious downward spiral of bad decision-making and *Heart-of-Hearts* feelings of low self-worth. Obviously, these are the undesirable consequences of poor and destructive choices caused by not having enough self-love in our *Heart-of-Hearts*.

- When our best judgment and cognitive processes are clouded, enveloped, and hijacked by our emotions, impulses, and urges, we oftentimes don't think and reason correctly; and as a direct result, we settle for making poor life choices and acting in a destructive manner. In many instances, in order to mitigate the power generated by our emotions, we opt for quick fixes and easy solutions. Instead, we would be far better off exercising appropriate discipline and taking the path that may initially be a bit harder or longer but that will ultimately lead us to make far better life choices and secure more satisfying results in the long term.

- Our toxic emotions can dismantle our best judgment at *Crunch Time!* when we make our life choices. We may then make poor, destructive, poisonous, and self-sabotaging choices. Therefore, we must master our emotions and impulses so our cognitive processes are free and clear when we make life choices. We then put ourselves in the best position to aspire higher—that is, to make life choices that reflect and effect our highest values and self—loving, respectful, compassionate, constructive choices that make us feel great about ourselves and our ability to bring about positive results and highly beneficial changes in our life and in the lives of others.

THE CONCEPT OF "E3"

Let's now discuss how you can master your emotions and impulses and have them work in harmony with your intellect, best judgment, and *Heart-of-Hearts* to equip, enable, and empower (or "E3") you to live the life you dream about as you assist others in living their best lives.

If you are going to aspire higher, be your best self, and fill your *Heart-of-Hearts* with feelings that will fuel you to do great things for yourself and others, you must be able to make toxic-emotion-free, cognitively clear decisions and choices.

EMOTION-GENERATED ENERGY CHARGES:
The Cognitive Versus the Emotional Components of Life Choices

Generally, when trying to understand emotions, we tend to view them from an intellectual standpoint. However, *The PLCP Lifestyle* studies the physiology of emotions, in that it focuses on the often highly potent energy charges these emotions trigger. For example, whereas we often think of the emotion of "love" in an intellectual sense, we rarely think of it as a catalyzing physiological force, and we almost never knowingly and strategically channel the exceedingly strong energy charges this emotion generates to our advantage.

To illustrate what I mean by the physiology of emotions, think about the huge adrenaline rush that you feel when something or someone triggers your anger or rage; how sky-high you feel and how supremely motivated you are when you're in love; or how incredibly excited you feel when you secure or attain something you've been dreaming of. You're charged up! For our purposes, what you feel in these instances are the energy charges generated by your strong emotions.

Mastering potentially sabotaging poisonous emotions and their energy charges is your *emotional imperative* if you aspire to elevate your life and the lives of those around you.

Years ago, I gave a speech about the "Components of Constructive Decision-Making." I discussed the concepts and formulas that I had developed to enable individuals to control, overpower, and ultimately nullify potentially destructive emotions when trying to make their most cognitively clear and wisest choices. At the end of my presentation, one of *Oprah*'s ex-producers approached me and essentially said, "All of the decision-making theories that I've heard in the past focus on the *intellectual* component of decision-making. But you deal with the *emotions*. And, while most of us intellectually *know* what we *should* do in a given situation, when strong emotions come into play, we often make terrible decisions. If you can show people how to separate their emotions from their decision-making [processes], you will be able to help a great many people and make a real contribution."

Besides offering much-appreciated encouragement, this magnanimous program executive also highlighted **two distinctly different influences that can play major roles when you make your life choices:**

- Your intellect (or what you know or think)

- Your emotions, urges, and impulses (what you feel)

As we shall discuss, these two influences can be at absolute odds when you make your life choices. However, as you will see, your intellect and emotions can indeed work in concert, enabling you to accomplish your most dearly held goals, live the life that you dream about, and enjoy the tremendously empowering and energizing feelings of making purposeful life choices.

YOUR EMOTIONAL
IMPERATIVE

Let's hearken back to the classic stimulus-response experiment conducted by I. P. Pavlov. As you may remember, Pavlov would introduce a piece of meat to a dog, and the dog would react by salivating. At some point, along with the introduction of the meat, the dog would hear the ringing of a bell. With repetition, the dog began to associate the sound of the bell with the luscious meat. This led to the dog salivating on cue, even when there was no meat in the vicinity. Therefore, Pavlov, through the effective use of positive reinforcement, was able to "condition" a predictable response from the dog. This was important early work in the field of behaviorism, and we will come back to it later in order to discuss its relevance in connection with mastering your emotions.

Thereafter, B. F. Skinner advanced the field of behaviorism by developing behavioral-conditioning theories for human beings that are based on our ability to elicit, to teach, and to learn certain desired human behaviors through the use of positive and negative reinforcement.

Dr. M. Scott Peck enlightened us a good deal further in his brilliant work, *The Road Less Traveled*. Therein, Dr. Peck essentially discussed and celebrated the all-important difference between the automatic reaction elicited from the dog in Pavlov's stimulus-response experiment and a human's ability to not simply react but, instead, to consciously and knowingly act when a stimulus is introduced.

Peck discussed the concept of "bracketing," which means that when we are exposed to a stimulus, instead of automatically reacting as Pavlov's pooch did, we as human beings have the ability to take a step back, think, and decide on an appropriate response.[1] According to Dr. Peck and Dr. Stephen Covey in his landmark book, *7 Habits of Highly Effective People*, our gift and ability to think and choose—instead of simply automatically reacting in or to a given situation—is what makes us human.[2]

I wholeheartedly agree with both Drs. Peck and Covey regarding this point. However, thinking alone is not enough when we want to make our most positive life choices, as we are often exposed to certain potentially poison-provoking people, events, or situations. In these instances, we are often helplessly "all too human" as we let our toxic emotions, urges, and impulses flood and overtake our intellect, and we wind up making self-sabotaging choices and acting in an ill-considered, damaging way. Therefore, it is not enough to just (attempt to) think in these emotion-filled situations, when our mental processes are severely weakened or totally dismantled. In these instances, you need to have learned to control and master your emotions (optimally before the dangerous scenario even occurs) and to make them work *for* you so that you can think and evaluate clearly and effectively. Developing a strategic system of thinking to keep you armed against attempts made against your integrity, highest values, and sense of right is critical.

So, while *The PLCP Lifestyle* embraces Dr. Peck's and Dr. Covey's optimistic perspectives regarding our ability to objectively evaluate people, things, and conditions when we make our choices, as you will glean, *The PLCP Lifestyle* advances our evolution. It not only acknowledges the cognitive component of making life choices, but it provides you with the essential addition of a set of tried-and-true *Steps* to tap into and efficaciously use your most potent emotion-generated energy charges. As a direct result, your wisest and best judgment will prevail when you make your all-important life choices.

Once again, in many instances when you are called upon to make a life choice, you will be flooded with intense, battling, conflicting emotions. Therefore, in making positive choices, you must not only know what you want to secure or accomplish with your choices (Part 3 of this book), but you must also be in control of your emotions if you want to make choices that reflect and are consistent with your most highly valued goals and ideals.

9

HOW TO VIEW YOUR EMOTIONS, URGES, AND IMPULSES

Emotions aren't necessarily good or bad per se; they are benefi-cial if they and their energy charges catalyze and compel you to make a positive and constructive life choice. Conversely, emotions, impulses, and urges are poisonous and sabotaging if they and their energy charges lead you to make a self-defeating or self-destructive life choice.

As you know, in many instances, the emotion of anger can trig-ger self-sabotaging behavior from the person who feels angry. For example, I once counseled a talented individual, "Bill," who had tremendous potential in his chosen field. However, he also had per-sistent anger-management issues and suffered related setbacks. For as many good things as Bill had accomplished at his job, he'd also experienced countless damaging moments—when Bill's emotional buttons were pushed, he would frequently "lose his head" and viciously blow up at others. Here's Bill's story:

Bill's employer appreciated his considerable talents and often protected him by downplaying Bill's well-documented work-related blow-ups. But one day, when Bill yet again lost his temper in an exceedingly ugly, vitriolic, and rage-filled manner with a highly regarded employee who threatened to quit if Bill wasn't immediately let go, the employer—in light of the prior, valid complaints of other employees against Bill—had no choice but to terminate Bill's employment. In this instance, in spite of the fact that Bill had exceptional talent and loved his chosen field, he clearly couldn't control his temper when certain individuals or situations triggered certain toxic emotions within him. Sadly, within a year, Bill lost another, lesser position with another firm for exactly the same reason: his anger-filled outbursts.

Bill then spent nearly two years applying for less prominent positions, at less desirable firms, with no success. Thereafter, with tremendous bitterness and regret, Bill continued to struggle, as he had to accept far less rewarding and lucrative positions outside of the field that he loved and was, in many ways, perfectly suited for.

As was the case with my friend Steve, this is a clear case in which the emotion of anger flooded and overpowered someone beyond all reason, thereby obliterating good judgment. At Bill's original firm, he was reprimanded numerous times for his ugly emotional outbursts. Each time, during discussions with the firm's human resources department, Bill claimed that he "clearly understood" that he couldn't vent his anger against his fellow employees; he *knew* that his outbursts had been promotion killing and, over time, had become job-threatening. In one of his final meetings with human resources, Bill calmly and with great contrition said to the head of that department, as well as to the company's president, that he had thought things through (after his series of anger-related transgressions) and would be "smarter" the next time something or someone upset him. He then convincingly argued that he truly valued being at such a well-respected firm and was pursuing his dream career there. Over and over again, Bill said that he *knew* what he needed to do in the future, which was to never again lose his temper or be demeaning or retaliatory toward others.

Because Bill said all the right things and seemed to truly grasp both what he'd done wrong in the past and what he needed to do differently in the future, the firm gave him "one last chance" to shape up—an opportunity that he blew only weeks later.

The fact that Bill knew what his mistakes were and how he needed to comport himself in the future made absolutely no difference when the high-voltage energy charges generated by his deep-seated anger triggered his unacceptable and self-sabotaging behavioral pattern. In this case, the emotion of anger and the incredibly powerful jolts of energy generated from it were indeed poisonous, derailing Bill's good intentions and best judgment, fueling his self-destructive behavior.

On the other hand, NFL Hall of Fame–bound quarterback Tom Brady was allegedly angry and felt disrespected because he wasn't drafted until the 199th pick, in the sixth round of the 2000 NFL draft. Allegedly, these turbo-charged feelings of anger fueled Brady to excel in every game he played and thereby demonstrate to the NFL executives how wrong they were to let him slip so far down in the draft. This observation received strong validation years ago by the well-respected ESPN sports analyst Sal Paolantonio, on Colin Cowherd's national radio show, as they discussed why the megastar Brady and the coach of the New England Patriots, Bill Belichick, have been able to win with such remarkable consistency year after year. At one point during the interview, Paolantonio offered this insight: "The rocket fuel of this country is [the feeling] of resentment. Brady was passed over [in the NFL draft]. Belichick was [greatly] underrated."[1]

The enlightening lesson here is that in these two cases, the potent energy charges generated by the same emotion—anger—triggered two very different forms of expression. In Bill's case, it catalyzed and caused him to act destructively, as he totally disregarded what he knew to be the right behavior for him. Conversely, apparently Tom Brady has made the highly beneficial choice to constructively channel his alleged highly potent feelings of anger on the field, in order to become, in many individuals' estimation, the best and most successful quarterback in NFL history.

The important insight here is that an emotion in and of itself is neither positive nor poisonous; rather, it is the expression of that emotion—that is, the act that a particular emotion triggers—that can be either beneficial or self-defeating and self-sabotaging. Therefore, whether you are consciously and strategically able to manage your emotions or you are taken hostage by them at *Crunch Time!* may well dictate whether you will make a positive life choice or a poisonous one, respectively.

Let's now focus on the feeling of love. In many instances, love can inspire and motivate individuals to act in wonderfully constructive ways, such as being thoughtful of and compassionate toward others, doing charitable work, and being an overall better person— all beautiful expressions of the energy charges that love generates. However, in other instances, the expression of the emotion of love can be self-sabotaging and self-defeating.

For example, I know a wonderful, kind girl, "Beth," who is blessed to have a tremendous amount of love in her heart and is very open about expressing it. The problem is that on occasion, because Beth is so in touch with her feelings and so prone to sharing them, she can express her love at inappropriate times. An illustration of this occurred when she met "Kent" on a blind date, which was set up by their mutual friend, "Kiera."

This date was one of Kent's first since emerging from a long-term relationship with someone he loved very much. Before the first date, Beth was told explicitly by Kiera that what Kent wanted and needed was to have a light and breezy dating life until he healed from his fiancée breaking up with him.

The problem here, according to Beth, was that it had been years since she'd found someone like Kent with whom she connected so quickly and deeply. As a result, after her third date with the handsome, funny, and evolved Kent, Beth not only felt incredible love in her heart, but with great ardor, she also expressed it to him. At this point in Kent's life, this was the last thing he wanted to hear and experience. What Kent dearly wanted was air and space; nevertheless, with the best of intentions, what Beth gave him was love-filled smothering. And the more Kent retreated, the more Beth tried to become an integral part of his life—until he felt that it became necessary to have "the talk" with Beth and tell her that he needed to cool it with her, as he wasn't at all ready for anything serious or structured so soon after his breakup.

I know Kent well, and a year or so later, he confided to me that had he met a "warm, sweet, smart girl like Beth years earlier," he would have been much more ready to consider being in a serious and committed relationship. He then added, "The timing [of meeting Beth] so soon [after my engagement ended] was terrible!"

In this instance, we see how the energy charges generated from an emotion such as love, which often triggers beneficial life choices and actions, instead triggered in Beth a series of self-defeating life choices and self-destructive acts.

So, here's the profound problem: Notwithstanding Beth's *clear knowledge* of Kent's recent history and current state of mind (that he was fresh out of a painful, unwanted breakup of his engagement, and what he needed at that point was air and space), the overwhelming energy charges generated from Beth's need to express her love and/or assuage her feelings of neediness or loneliness totally overpowered her best judgment. The result was that she did the one thing that she would never knowingly want to do: drive away someone in whom she was romantically interested.

In review, there are **five important points** to reinforce here:

- An emotion itself isn't necessarily positive or negative. It is the act that an emotion triggers that is either positive and beneficial or poisonous and self-sabotaging.

- The expression of an emotion can make all the difference as to whether you have a self-esteem-raising result or a self-defeating, self-esteem-lowering one.

  An example of this can be seen in the case of Bill, whom we discussed earlier. The fact that Bill felt rage in the workplace was not the problem. What caused his termination was his uncontrolled and inappropriate expression of those feelings. You absolutely must be continually cognizant of the fact that it is one thing to feel the energy charges generated by a potentially poisonous emotion, but quite another to allow those feelings and their particular energy charges to trigger uncontrolled, self-sabotaging actions on your part. Had Beth kept her intense feelings in check and given Kent his requested space, the couple might still be together today. What derailed their relationship was Beth's uncontrolled expression of her emotions.

- What can be a poisonous expression of an emotion or urge in one case might not be in another situation. The expression's nature depends upon the context. Therefore, you must always strive to be astutely aware of the appropriate time and place to express a particular feeling or impulse. Had Beth waited until a more appropriate time to express her strong feelings for Kent, this expression may well have been received in a positive manner instead of in a negative one.

- You can only be consistently astute and discerning at choice-making time if you are in control of your emotions, so that you can think, intuit, evaluate, and reason with crystal clarity.

    The other day, my exceedingly wise friend and mentor, Don Browne, mentioned to me that in navigating your career, you need to "take the right risks, at the right times." Clearly implied in this insightful statement is that in order to know or correctly intuit the right risks and the right times to take them, you must be able to think, reason, and evaluate with crystal clarity and, therefore, be free of any potentially toxic emotions that could cloud or derail your best judgment.

- I often use the term "potentially toxic emotions," because an emotion is only toxic if it leads you to make a poor or bad choice and act in a counterproductive or destructive manner. However, if through the *PLCP* process of "Emotion and Impulse Management" (EIM), which we will soon discuss, you significantly dissipate or negate the power and efficacy of your toxic emotions and impulses, make a positive life choice, and act consistently with that choice, then no harm will be done. Therefore, the emotions that you experience in a given situation are only potentially toxic, depending upon how artfully you deal with and nullify them and their potency.

EMOTION AND IMPULSE MANAGEMENT (EIM)

*Effectively managing your
emotions and impulses is essential
if you are to live your very
best and highest life!*

—KL

As making cognitively clear, positive life choices is your goal, let's discuss the *PLCP* 9 Steps of Emotion and Impulse Management or "EIM." Optimally, what you want to accomplish is to master the art of making beneficial life choices free of emotions and impulses that can trigger you to make poor, destructive, or poisonous decisions. You will then be able to substantially elevate the quality of your life and inner confidence to effect great change in your life and raise your feelings of self-worth. Here are your Emotion and Impulse Management Steps so you can effectively deal with an onslaught of potentially poisonous emotions and/or impulses when you're making a choice:

STEP ONE

One of the best ways not to fall prey or succumb to a toxic emotion barrage at decision-making time is to predetermine what your decision will be. By doing this, you have a definite plan of action or "POA" at *Crunch Time!* when you're called upon to make a cognitively clear, positive life choice. A highly effective way to predetermine your decision involves the "Prevent Offense." In pro football, when a team is winning and wants to protect its lead late in the game, it often uses a strategy called a "prevent defense." Essentially, this is a defense designed to, at worst, give up midsized gains by the opponent but not to allow a "big play" that can result in the team that was leading the contest to lose it.

The Prevent Offense is an anticipatory and a preparatory step taken hours, days, or weeks before you are called on to make a life choice or series of life choices. Your explicit goal in employing the Prevent Offense is to have the intellectual clarity to consciously choose to make a life choice that is positive and self-image elevating. Depending upon the circumstances, you can prepare a POA or decision ahead of time so that you put yourself in the best position to secure the result at *Crunch Time!* that you are hoping for and envisioning.

Now, let's discuss the two forms of anticipation, "specific" and "general," and your two potential POAs, which are to be either *resolute* or *flexible,* respectively. Let's take the case that, at some point in the future, you will attend a party and be asked if you want an alcoholic beverage when you're the designated driver that evening for you and your friends; in anticipation of this event, you can prepare an ironclad response of "No, thank you, I'm driving." What this presupposes is that you are able to anticipate that a SPECIFIC event will take place—you being offered alcohol when you will be driving later in the evening. Knowing this, you decide in advance what your resolute answer will be, no matter what: "No, thanks, but no." There is no flexibility or deviation in this instance; you have a locked-in decision for this situation and you stick with it no matter what. This has been a hugely successful strategy for me when it came to losing weight, being disciplined to eat the right and healthy foods throughout my life, breaking bad habits or sabotaging behavioral scripts, and the like.

On the other hand, pretend you are a college student and you have exams to study for this weekend. The optimal option would be to spend the whole weekend studying and not go out with anyone. That said, if that potentially "special guy/girl" who you met last week were to ask you out or your parents were to visit you, as they said they might, you need the flexibility that in certain instances, you may well change your premade plans of not going out. In this case, since some factors are unknown—and therefore, you can't specifically anticipate the variables that you will be called upon to deal with at *Crunch Time!*—your premade decision needs to be more flexible.

Years ago, I heard an ESPN Radio interview with the highly successful former USC football coach Pete Carroll, who was talking about how the USC football team would prepare for their upcoming big games. Coach Carroll discussed general and specific anticipation. He essentially said: "We always prepare for the known [the specific] and the unknown [the general]. Often, it's how you handle the unknown that will determine your success. We always prepare well. This gives us the best chance to deal with both the known and the unknown."[1]

According to Coach Carroll, if you prepare correctly and thoroughly, the chances are far greater that you will act and react most effectively at *Crunch Time!* to both the factors and events that you can specifically anticipate and those you can't. Following Coach Carroll's insight, if you can efficaciously prepare for future situations where you will be called upon to make a choice, you will be able to lock in that beneficial choice ahead of time and then recall and visualize that choice at *Crunch Time!* and act on it. You can thereby negate the potentially toxic emotionally driven energy charges that might lead you to otherwise make a poor decision.

STEP TWO

Do not make a major decision, unthinkingly react to a person or event, or figuratively or literally press the "send button" when you are enveloped and hijacked by potentially toxic emotions and impulses or when you feel "emotionally off." Stop whatever you're doing, relax, and take whatever time you need to cool down. Take a few long, deep breaths. Step away from the heat, angst, and seemingly compelling needs of the moment, and wait until calm, serenity, and clarity return.

STEP THREE

This step is devoted to dissipating and thereby negating the potency of the potentially poisonous emotion-generated energy charges that are hijacking you and dismantling your best judgment. Once the strength of the energy charges has been significantly diminished, you are then able to think and reason with far more clarity and precision, thereby paving the way for you to make highly positive and constructive life choices.

By way of illustration, let me explain the process of Toxic Energy Charge Dissipation (TECD). I remember a case where I admired how my wise and kind executive assistant, Shari Freis, attentively and compassionately listened to a client unload over the phone all of her professionally related frustrations with her employer. After about forty-five minutes of venting, the client calmed down and thereafter thanked Shari for being such a gracious and supportive listener and sounding board.

After that call, I asked Shari why she spent so much of her valuable time listening as did. She responded, "Because, if the client purges with me, they run out of steam, and their frustration and anger levels significantly lessen. So, when they later talk with you, they are much more relaxed, as well as far more focused on and clear about what they really need to accomplish."

"You are truly brilliant, Shari," I told her.

This form of negative energy release or venting is similar to the process of Toxic Energy Charge Dissipation. The purging allows the clients to rid themselves of the frustration, angst, anger, or fear that they have allowed to flood them and their cognitive processes. Afterward, in a cool, calm, and clear manner, they are able to reason, evaluate, and strategize. Similarly, if you are able to significantly dissipate the "steam" and potency of your potentially poisonous emotions, you will then be able to think clearly, exercise your best judgment, and make life choices that reflect your highest and wisest self.

Some highly effective ways to dissipate the strength of the potentially poisonous emotions that are hijacking you, cool down, and regain your composure and cognitive clarity are to:

- Make a *Blessing List* and visualize all of the good things in your life.

  For example, here is a *Blessing List* that I made when I needed to calm down and dissipate the potency of the potentially poisonous emotions that were enveloping me:

  a. I have a beautiful, loving wife, son, and daughter whom I deeply love and am abundantly blessed to have in my life.

  b. I'm blessed to be healthy.

c. I love my life and recognize that these truly are and will be remembered as "the good old days" and they are to be cherished.

d. I love our three adorable doggies.

e. I love our home and all of the wonderful big and small events over the years that we've shared there.

f. I love playing tennis with my wife and playing POP Tennis with my friends.

g. I love my work, my writing, and being of service to others.

h. I'm truly blessed in so many ways.

In almost all instances, by the time I finish making my *Blessing List* and review it, I've calmed down considerably and, soon thereafter, cognitive clarity returns.

- Find love in your *Heart-of-Hearts* and express that love in your upcoming life choice(s).

- Find forgiveness for yourself and others in your *Heart-of-Hearts*, and express this forgiveness in your life choice(s).

- Make an authentic effort to truly understand the reasons why relevant others act as they do and to also understand their backgrounds and personal histories. Figuratively, try to walk a mile in others' shoes. Be insightfully and lovingly understanding of yourself and of others so that you can understand where you and others are coming from and incorporate this knowledge into your choice-making processes.

In connection with points 3 and 4 above, I would like to hearken back to the story I shared with you about how deeply hurt by and angry I was with my dad during the first few years of my life because I incorrectly felt that he didn't love me. As I discussed, I was so intensely angry with my dad when I was four years old that I tossed a brick at him. Thankfully, my aim was as bad as my judgment, as I missed hitting him by a wide margin.

As I discussed earlier, it wasn't until I reached eleven or twelve years old that I began to truly understand the compelling reasons why my dad didn't seem to be there for me during my early years and why he wasn't able to effectively communicate with me. Just after I was born, my parents made an agreement that my mom would stay home with me and that my father would support us. As a result, he had to work six long days a week and many nights in order for my parents to afford for my mom to stay home with me full-time and for me to enjoy an excellent education. Additionally, my dad's father died when my dad was young, so he grew up without the father whom he dearly loved. As a result, my dad had no fathering role model to emulate. So, he didn't know how to express his deep love for me.

Once I learned and was old enough to understand and truly appreciate these realities, the poisonous emotional energy charges within me that had been triggered by my dad's seeming unloving behavior quickly dissipated. In place of the feelings of hurt, rejection, and anger that I initially felt were feelings for my dad of forgiveness, compassion, and sympathy for having lost his loving father at such an early age. These feelings were coupled with my sincere appreciation of and pure, strong love for my dad. As time passed and my dad and I got to spend more time together, all of these positive, loving feelings grew and became deeply entrenched in my *Heart-of-Hearts*; these feelings figuratively pushed out and replaced the highly potent emotion-generated energy charges of the burning anger and hurt that once enveloped me.

All this to say, learning about, understanding, and respecting where someone has been (their experiences and burdens) or is coming from, and showing understanding, compassion, and empathy for that person can go a long way in empowering you to dissipate the potency of the potentially toxic emotions that you are dealing with and are embedded in your *Heart-of-Hearts*.

I often recall a freezing cold day years ago as I was walking around Manhattan. All sorts of things were irking me. And just as I was about to commence my internal pity party, I saw a blind, homeless man sleeping on the cold street. At his side was a cardboard sign that read "Blind, homeless, and starving U.S. Vet. Please help!"

As I absorbed this devastatingly sad reality, my heart ached terribly. I approached that gentleman, put money into his cup, and brought him a hot meal. Upon saying goodbye to him, I thought, *What could I possibly be unhappy or agitated about?* As I walked away, I had already forgotten the truly insignificant issues that had been upsetting me that day. Finding and expressing compassion and empathy can truly put things in their proper perspective.

As we wrap up this step, I want to share a poem I wrote about how helpful a *Blessing List* can be when I want to escape from the heat and angst of the moment and avoid a downward emotional spiral:

NEGATIVE TOWN AND THE EFFECT OF
THE NEGATIVITY BIAS

When things upset me and bring me down,
And I quickly head to Negative Town.
I recall my blessings and they make me feel,
That what I'm facing, isn't such a bad deal.

With this more positive mindset, I'll be constructive,
And not go to a place that's so self-destructive.

And thereby not listen to my negative voices,
As I endeavor to make my very best choices.
So, when things don't go as you want them to,
And when negativity seeps in as it's wont to do,
I visualize my blessings and then write them down,
So I don't take a trip to Negative Town.

STEP FOUR

Remember and vividly visualize the instances when you made self-diminishing and damaging life choices in the past and you wound up regrettably taking the low road because you were caught in the vortex of poisonous emotions, such as anger, rage, hate, jealousy, insecurity, hurt, desperation, and insecurity. When you do this, your explicit goal is to avoid making the same misstep again; instead, you want to make a cognitively clear, toxic emotion–free choice that reflects your highest values. Visualizing yourself making a past highly constructive and/or beneficial action can also assist you in achieving that clarity.

STEP FIVE

Be "Consequence Cognizant": Consider the most severe and heinous consequences that could occur if you act out of impulse; and then visualize the negative or even tragic effects that your reckless acts could have on you and your loved ones, or anyone or anything that matters to you.

STEP SIX

Remind yourself that you want complete intellectual clarity and cognitive precision when you make your life choices. *You* want to be in control and call the shots—not your emotions!

I remember years ago, each day I'd walk my adorable Maltese puppy, Peanut, down our block as one of our neighbors, "Al," would often speed down the block, racing to get home from work. His reckless and thoughtless driving always scared me, as children play and dogs get walked in our normally tranquil neighborhood. Then one day, Al sped home as usual, this time nearly running sweet Peanut over. I was fuming! However, I did my best to calm myself down, knowing that if I became aggressive and yelled at my unthinking neighbor, he would inevitably become defensive and not hear me. Instead, I decided to take control of my emotions and the situation, walk over to Al, and do my best to connect with him in a manner that would foster him truly listening to me and absorbing the gravity of the situation.

As he was getting out of his car, I said, "Al, how are you?" He responded, "Oh, I'm frazzled and slammed. I'm litigating this case . . . it's going terribly, and my client's really upset with me! It's a real mess!" I could see that Al was quite troubled; I decided to slow down to process what I might say to him so that he would truly hear me and react appropriately. A moment later, I began, "Oh, I'm so sorry. I've had situations like that and they're never fun. Let's hope things go much better tomorrow. Al, I know that you're preoccupied with your case, but you almost hit and killed little Peanut, and I know that your two beautiful children also play on the block. Can you imagine someone speeding down our block and hitting either Zack or Jenna?"

Al took a long moment to visualize such a horrible occurrence, and then said in a much warmer tone, "I'm so sorry, Kenny. I certainly wouldn't want to hurt Peanut or see my kids injured. I've just been so wrapped up in this horrible case for months that I can't wait to get home. It's my refuge. I so appreciate you letting me know about my driving. I wasn't thinking. I definitely will drive slower and be more in the moment. Thanks so much!"

Interestingly, not only did Al drive much more slowly down our block thereafter, but we became pretty good friends as a result of our talk. So, my being in control of my emotions and the situation at *Crunch Time!* secured two favorable results.

STEP SEVEN

Ask yourself: "As I weigh my most important values, what do I want to accomplish with this life choice?"; "What kind of person do I truly aspire to be?"; and "How do I aspire higher or highest with this life choice and my actions?"

STEP EIGHT

Next, be aware that making life choices is like playing chess, in that one move or choice can very well impact moves and choices that you will be called upon to make days, weeks, or years later. So, it's essential that when you are making your life choices to view them through the long-term, big-picture lens of living your best and highest life and being your best and highest self.

This way, you will remain clearly cognizant at *Crunch Time!* of your preeminent values and your biggest and most treasured goals and dreams, and make choices and decisions that are consistent with and reflective of them. By doing this you also take strong steps to be appropriately disciplined and not settle for the immediate gratification of making a choice or decision that makes you feel good for the moment, but may be counter to or preclude you from achieving your long-term goals and living your ultimate dreams.

Always remember, practicing the arts of being disciplined and delaying gratification at the right times, until you can receive a far more valuable and *Heart-of-Hearts* fulfilling payoff, can elevate your life in the most wonderful and game-changing ways. Don't settle . . . aspire higher!

STEP NINE

Make the most positive, beneficial, and constructive choice or decision for yourself and for those whose lives your choice or decision will impact.

REVIEW YOUR
LIFE-CHOICE-MAKING
PROCESS

Now that *Crunch Time!* has passed and you've made your life choice, you want to objectively and honestly review whether you are happy with the decision you've made. If the answer is yes, acknowledge and celebrate it. However, if you feel that you didn't perform as well as you could have at *Crunch Time!*—and we *all* have times when we feel this way—then identify what went wrong and get it right for the next *Crunch Time!* This process becomes your first step to getting your next life choice–making opportunity to be a far more positive and rewarding experience.

Let's focus on the case when you did in fact make a positive life choice at *Crunch Time!*

Once you have made a beneficial life choice, acknowledge it, enjoy it, and let your wonderful accomplishment truly resonate within you. This is a key process for you, because, when you effectively master your emotions and their energy charges and then make a *positive* life choice, the result is incredibly empowering. Taking your fate into your capable hands and choice-by-choice creating the life you've dreamed about is empowering. To own your choices and your destiny is empowering. To truly know that you can consistently accomplish *all of this* is empowering! And all of these high-self-esteem-building feelings generate supremely powerful positive energy charges that you can store in your *Heart-of-Hearts*. As a result, when you are faced with making future life choices and your negativity bias stealthily attempts to impact you and your thought processes, you can draw upon these highly potent stored positive feelings to motivate and lead you to make more and increasingly better choices.

Once you have made your positive life choice, the following are some highly beneficial acts to assist you in keeping your *Heart-of-Hearts* filled with your most potent, positive perceptions of yourself and your ability to truly effect positive change in your life:

Acknowledge and be proud of the fact that you made a life choice in such an effective manner, that you were able to aspire higher as you attained your goals.

Celebrate and savor a life choice well-thought-out, well-executed, and made free from the sabotaging emotion-generated energy charges that might normally have clouded or derailed your best judgment. Feel and enjoy your triumph and your power. The more you feel and enjoy your accomplishments, the more they will energize and motivate you to make many more *brilliant* life choices in the future. This is so because you've seen and enjoyed the extremely beneficial results of your life-choice-making, and you feel in your *Heart-of-Hearts* that you and your bright future are worth making *positive* life choices for. This concept reflects B. F. Skinner's theory of behaviorism as we tend to seek out more and more positive, feel-good experiences.

Now let's discuss how to correct your *Crunch Time!* stumbles, to improve and enhance your future *Crunch Time!* life-choice-making experiences.

THE STUMBLE

When performing the *9 Steps of Emotion and Impulse Management*, never lose sight of the following core concept:

As human beings, we have the abilities to think, value, reason, learn, grow, evolve, and attain tremendous heights. But being human, we will also make mistakes, stumble, and suffer setbacks. Learning to constructively pick yourself up after stumbles is part of everyone's growth process. In connection with this process, I'd like to share a personal story with you.

At sixteen, I became a successful East Coast junior tennis player. During that year, I entered a New York City men's tournament. After defeating a couple of opponents, I was pitted against a top-ranked East Coast player who at age thirty-five had a great deal of experience and tournament savvy. He was left-handed and had a wicked serve that spun off the court in a manner that was totally opposite from that of a right-hander.

I had never competed against a truly talented left-handed player before. The problem was not only that his shots and spin were coming from a different angle than I was used to, but every time I expected to approach the net on his weaker backhand, I wound up approaching on his excellent forehand instead. I'd forget he was a lefty. I was all crossed up.

He trounced me, 6–1, 6–1. What was worse was that he had confounded me. I seemed at a total loss as to how to beat him.

After the match and for a few days thereafter, I was down in the dumps and felt that all of the air had been let out of my spiritual balloon. My confidence hit rock bottom. Thank goodness, my mother put things in their proper perspective by helping me see the big picture of what had happened and what had to be done to remedy the situation. She observed that I had never played such a good and polished left-hander before, and that I needed to learn how to play against and adjust my game to left-handers. We then decided to find a left-handed tennis coach to teach me, which turned out to be a constructive decision.

We found a great coach, George Seewagen, who explained concepts to me in a manner that I could understand and implement. After about a year of practice, hard work, and improvement, I came up against the same left-handed opponent again. With a different perspective, better footwork, and a more complete arsenal of weapons, I defeated him fairly decisively, 6–3, 6–2. More importantly, I no longer had trouble adjusting to left-handed players.

After the match, I reflected on the fact that the loss to the left-hander a year earlier had seemed to be a devastating stumble when it happened. But I now realized that it had identified a glaring flaw in my game that needed to be fixed. That devastating loss triggered a positive and necessary corrective decision and action on my part. Now I was lying in bed, feeling great about my day's victory. As it turned out, my seemingly horrible loss was my *first big step* toward developing a better all-around game and securing many more elating future victories. Or, put more succinctly: I stumbled; I was humbled; but then, with the right improvements, I rumbled. Sweet!

As we discussed earlier, every time you compete in anything, you run the risk of losing or not coming out on top. Additionally, in order to truly self-actualize, there will be many times when you can or will try new things and push the proverbial envelope to see what you are capable of accomplishing; this is how you increase and enhance your behavioral repertoire and your confidence to continue to attempt new things. Realize and be at peace with the reality that whenever you embark on an endeavor, you may stumble, hit a road-block, or not secure the result you were hoping for. It's part and parcel of living an active and purposeful life of learning, growing, evolving, and aspiring higher.

I have also learned that the acts of winning and losing are in many respects illusions and not at all as they seem. A saying posted outside the All-England Club, home of Wimbledon, reads: "If you can meet with Triumph and Disaster, and treat those two impos-tors just the same . . ."[1] What I believe Rudyard Kipling meant when he gave that sage advice was that if you choose to adopt the mindset of perceiving both winning and losing as highly bene-ficial means of learning and growing, and not as ends in and of themselves, you will be the real winner in the long run, as you will secure the true big W: Wisdom.

The final thoughts for you to keep in mind here are: One or two raindrops do not a flood make; a couple of snowflakes do not a blizzard make; a few pebbles do not an avalanche make; and one or two mistakes or stumbles do not generally an irreparable situation or catastrophe make. And, in almost all cases, there is always tomor-row and many more opportunities down the road to make highly beneficial choices that will get you and your life on a more positive and far better track.

No matter how evolved, smart, or talented we are, we will *never* do everything perfectly every time. In fact, I have observed that so many individuals become angst and fear ridden, demoralized, and intellectually and emotionally paralyzed because they seek unattainable perfection. The debilitating result is that they never feel like they are "good enough," they often feel "less than," and they are never satisfied with their work, efforts, or result. Obviously, this can be a serious long-term problem. I suggest that you don't seek perfection, but rather do and be the best that you are capable of and be happy when you accomplish this great, empowering goal. Also, please remember that sustained and highly rewarding success is attained by doing the "right" things as much of the time as possible and to come up *big* when your most cherished *values, goals, and dreams* are at stake.

CORRECTION DAY

As we discussed in the previous chapter, you won't be able to make every life choice to your ideal specifications. You will occasionally experience flaws in your Emotion and Impulse Management process or your follow-through, in that you won't always take actions that are consistent with your ideal life choices. As a result, at some point after you make your life choice and act or refrain from acting, it will be time to reflect upon and fix what might have gone wrong or what you could have done better. The perfect time to do this is when you are able to reflect and clearly see—poisonous-emotion-generated, energy-charge-free—what truly transpired. This way, you're dealing with the honest, unobstructed truth.

Years ago, I was listening to ESPN Radio when I heard a college football player talk about the Monday following the team's Saturday game. That player basically said that Monday was *Correction Day* for the team. This meant that now that the dust had settled and the intense heat of their battle had cooled, it was the best time for the players and the coaching staff to carefully and nondefensively study the videotapes from Saturday's game.

Their **correction day goals** were to:

- Identify and fix their flaws and missteps, and examine the things that they could improve upon so that they would be better equipped to secure sweet victories in their upcoming games.

- Identify the things that they did well—and see if they could execute them even better so that they could continue to capitalize on these skills and assets in the future.

As important as it is for you to acknowledge, celebrate, savor, enjoy, and feel your life-choice victories so that you are able to fill your *Heart-of-Hearts with positives*, it is equally important to honestly and nondefensively identify and acknowledge how you could have done things better or more skillfully so that you don't make the same missteps again when you're presented with your next similar choice-making opportunity.

Always remember that everyone occasionally stumbles when endeavoring to master their emotions and/or make their life choices.

The keys, **when you do make a mistake or you could have done something better,** are to:

- Honestly and nondefensively identify the misstep.

- Visualize it.

- Figure out *how* to be more effective when you make your future life choices.

- Do your best not to repeat the same misstep in the future.

- Engage in what I call "selective amnesia" in that you want to learn from your mistake or misstep and carry that valuable insight with you moving forward, but you don't want to continue to be brought down or demoralized by it. So you selectively remember the life lesson but leave the negative experience in your rearview mirror as you constructively drive toward securing many sweet future successes!

One final thought is that it's always beneficial and life-enhancing to learn and improve from your mistakes, but in some cases, an equally beneficial strategy is not to make a misstep in the first place. If you are able to make cognitively clear choices and, as we will discuss in Part 3 that follows, be focused on making choices that reflect your highest values and aspirations, you significantly increase your chances that you can preempt or negate a potential life choice faux pas.

Part 3

Know What Your Highest Values and Goals Are

14

YOUR GOLD AND TRUTH

To thine own self be true.
—WILLIAM SHAKESPEARE,
Hamlet

Now that we have discussed how you can instill positive feelings of self-love and love for others into your *Heart-of-Hearts* and make cognitively clear life choices by managing your potentially toxic emotions, let's focus on the process of identifying your highest and preeminent values and goals. Or, stated another way, as an ever-evolving individual, please identify your **gold and truth goals:**

- What do you want the most for and in your life (your "gold")?

- What kind of person do you most aspire to be (your "truth")?

Effectively answering these questions involves your valuation—that is, learning or confirming what you value most for yourself, your happiness and your well-being, and for others.

As a means to illustrate the process of insightful valuation, I'd like to share two personal stories with you.

Years ago, when I was single, I had the opportunity to open up a New York City–based television news and hosting representation office to go along with the one we enjoy in Los Angeles. There was no question in my mind that we would have been hugely successful with a Manhattan office, as long as I spent a good deal of time there each month. It also would have been quite lucrative for us. The downside to opening that office was that I would be going back and forth between coasts on a regular basis. So, I had to evaluate the pros and the cons of making such a dramatic life and professional change.

The positives to opening up the office were that we would sign more, highly attractive New York City–based clients, as New York City was the largest local TV market in the country, and the network news divisions were based there. Additionally, because we had choreographed the steps for a great many of our news clients to secure major hosting positions, we would be an attractive agency for many East Coast–based newscasters who would like to become hosts and for those who would at least like to seriously consider that option. So, we would increase our top-drawer client list and our profitability.

The negatives were that I didn't want to compromise or significantly diminish the time that I spent being athletic and enjoying the beautiful Los Angeles weather. I had spent many years working six or seven days a week starting and growing my company, and I had sacrificed much of my personal time and enjoyment doing so. I was highly reluctant to do it all over again by having to staff and run a new office and build a business in New York City. I realized that traveling every couple weeks across the country would be a real physical and emotional drain on me. I also acknowledged that I was doing well financially with just an LA office, so the extra money that I would earn wasn't a necessity, just a luxury. I also remembered the profound and impactful thought that my father shared with me many years earlier when, after his astute valuation, he chose not to accept a lucrative opportunity to leave his excellent position at the department store chain that he was working for, to start his own department store chain. "Kenny," he told me, "I never want to be the richest guy in the cemetery. The ones you love, your health, true happiness—*they're* important!"

Upon doing my valuation, I realized that my preeminent values were protecting and making the most of my free time, my physical and mental health, and the excellent work-life balance that I had finally achieved. Knowing this, I wisely opted not to open a New York City office.

DON'T SELL OUT WHEN IT COMES TO HAPPINESS

Years later, I was approached by a number of talent agencies inquiring whether I'd be interested in selling my agency to them and becoming a major executive with their stellar, full-service agency. Once again, I went through my valuation process, which was relatively easy. I loved spending time with my wonderful wife, daughter, son, and three adorable doggies. By owning my agency, I enjoyed the blessing and luxury of being able to call my own shots, such as when I start my day, when I finish my day, and how I allocate my time—elements that filled my *Heart-of-Hearts* with happy and hugely empowering feelings of freedom and autonomy. What this meant to me, more specifically, was that whenever I wanted to spend time with my family, such as have lunch or play tennis with my wife, or I needed to drive our kids to school, pick them up, be available for them for a cross-country meet or a get-together at a friend's house, I could make myself available. No one was watching over me or telling me that I had to attend this meeting or that.

The freedom that I treasure had become my overriding value. Knowing this has made it easy to quickly evaluate incoming offers to buy my agency and graciously decline them. At this point in my life and valuation, the freedom to be with my family when I choose is my most important value.

CONTROL YOUR PATH

Throughout my counseling career, I've been surprised at the incredibly large number of people who don't take the necessary time or make the all-important effort to search deep down in their *Heart-of-Hearts* in order to ascertain what it is that they truly want to accomplish and the kind of person that they would most like to be during their precious lifetime. I have found that many individuals seek and are more comfortable with being continually busy so that they don't have the time to truly take stock of their lives. As a result, they don't have to face the stark reality of how far they've strayed from their *Heart-of-Hearts*, truest desires, having severely compromised their goals and dreams, their ideals, and/or themselves. As a result, most of these individuals are unfocused and directionless. It's no wonder why so many people feel lost, empty, rudderless, and unsatisfied. How can they feel truly fulfilled and that they are living a purpose-focused life if they haven't taken the time to learn what they truly want and who they aspire to be?

Years ago, I knew a young man who chose his high school, many of his activities, his college, and his career based upon what his mother envisioned and wanted for him. He was her puppet. What this mother did was to intellectually and psychologically cripple her son, because he had come to rely so much on her planning and running his life that when he was put in the position to have to make choices for himself, he was totally lost. He had no vision, plans, or aspirations of his own, and he had zero confidence that he could make the right decisions and effectively execute them. As a result, even after his mother passed, this individual was helpless when it came to setting goals for himself. Sadly, he floundered throughout his life.

I have also seen many instances where individuals feel that the attainment of what they want and the person they aspire to be presents such a daunting undertaking that they become paralyzed by fear, timid, and/or depressed just thinking about their heartfelt goals and dreams. This potentially destructive behavior is often caused by the way these individuals were raised, by the real or perceived rejection or nonsuccesses that they have experienced in the past, and/or by their negativity bias. As a result, these individuals are afraid to put themselves, their hopes, and their aspirations on the line for fear of failure. Or they are afraid to succeed, as they feel that one day they may be exposed as not truly having the talent or other goods to warrant their success; this phenomenon is commonly referred to as "impostor syndrome."[1]

PUT THE PERCENTAGES IN YOUR FAVOR THAT YOU WILL ATTAIN YOUR GOALS

The insightful examination as to what your highest and most important values are is an ongoing process, for with the passage of time, your values, goals, and perception of self may well change.

Unquestionably, I have found that the individuals who know who they are, achieve their goals, and are genuinely fulfilled are the ones who take the following **steps to significantly increase their chances that they will attain their goals:**

- They take the requisite time to search deep down to truly learn who they are; what makes them happy, excited, and inspired; and the person they most aspire to be.

- They have a strong sense of what they want.

- They can visualize their goal attainment. ("If you can see it, you can far more easily be it.")

- They have the core confidence and belief that their goal is indeed attainable. ("You won't achieve it, if you don't believe it.")

- They have a game plan or choreography as to how to attain their goals.

- They know that as time passes, their values, goals, and aspirations regarding the kind of person they most want to be may change, so what they include in their *Lists*, which we will discuss in depth below, or the order of the items on those *Lists* may change. So, they take time whenever it's appropriate to amend their *Lists* so that their *Lists* accurately reflect their most current, preeminent values, goals, and aspirations.

As someone who wants to achieve their goals and make the most of their life, starting today, identifying what you truly desire for your life must be a major priority. I promise that it will give you big-picture vision, clarity, direction, and focus—all qualities that supremely successful goal achievers have developed. Sadly, I have witnessed many individuals who did not take the time to identify their major goals; as a result, they wasted lots of time flailing around, missing the mark, and being directionless. Instead, they could have maximized their time, energy, efforts, and life by taking logical, direct, success-evoking steps to attain their goals and live their dreams and establishing a clear vision of what they want. Please remember that if you constantly flail, you'll probably fail to truly fulfill your greatest potentials and find true *Heart-of-Hearts* happiness, peace, and fulfillment.

By visualizing what you truly want, having the discipline to stay on the often difficult course of going for your dreams and not opting for the immediate gratification of less satisfying substitutes will be far easier. Your goals are to go for—and achieve—a highest-value-driven, purposeful life, full self-actualization, heart-filling fulfillment, strong feelings of self-love and self-confidence, and valid pride regarding the person you have worked hard to evolve into.

A key to identifying what you most want in your life and the person whom you truly want to be is being laser-focused on what you want and not on what your parents, spouse, partner, friends, employer, and others want for you or expect of you. In order to accomplish this goal, you must commit the necessary time and energy to find a quiet place that allows you to decompress and break through the clutter of everything that is swirling around in your mind. I do this by taking long walks on the beach, bike rides, scenic hikes, or by sitting quietly in a favorite, comfortable place. The prettier the scenery, the quieter and calmer the surroundings, and the fewer distractions, the better. Find a place that transports you, moves you, inspires you, calms you, and encourages you to be introspective and appreciative.

Once you're there, think about what would put a smile in your *Heart-of-Hearts* and on your face. Visualize a goal or life that energizes you and captures your imagination. Ask yourself: "What would make my heart and soul sing?" Dare to contemplate your truest and most wonderful dreams—no matter how far-fetched or distant they may appear.

Let your thoughts and imagination run wild, and allow your

Heart-of Hearts to well up with an anticipation and visualization of what can be—as exciting ideas and dreams come to mind. Feel like a kid again—back to a time when no boundaries or impediments concerned you.

This contemplation process is essential if you want to live a life that is true to and reflective of who you are and the life you most want to live. When you are happy and in harmony with your life choices and the life you've made for yourself, you will be far healthier spiritually, mentally, emotionally, and physically, as the mind-spirit-body connection has proven to be strong.

Please keep in mind that even the most successful achievers have fallen short many times when endeavoring to fulfill their goals and dreams. For example, Abraham Lincoln is often cited for losing a number of elections before he was eventually elected president.

As impressive as Lincoln becoming president is, even more remarkable is that he suffered numerous crushing defeats and setbacks, along with the death of his sweetheart and a nervous breakdown, yet he never gave up his quest for and dream of being president. Each time he was knocked down and had the emotional wind knocked out of his sails, he dusted himself off and got back in the race until he eventually won it.

As you go through your examination process and dig deep within, you may well feel pangs of sadness. This is part of your process. Pondering aspirations compromised or unfulfilled, and valuable time seemingly wasted and lost can produce deep pain. But be heartened and excited by the fact that you're now on your way to knowing what you truly want in and for your life. You can now become the person you have always wanted to be. Begin now to envision the *great* things that you can and will attain and enjoy by taking the time to identify your truest values, goals, and dreams.

Know also that your initial examination process may easily require days, weeks, or months of spending quiet time in order to uncover what you cherish most. So lovingly give yourself all of the ultra-important, enlightening, and beneficial exploration time that you need. By doing this you engage in true self-love and highly efficacious self-help. The following poem may inspire you. Be excited and highly optimistic, and have fun as you immerse yourself in mining, exploring, and identifying what you sincerely want. Once you discover your truth, you've taken a huge step toward living it.

DISCERNING WHAT YOU REALLY WANT

If you want to know what lies deep inside,
You must drop your defenses and no longer hide;
And become the most effective sleuth,
By searching your heart and discerning the truth.
Don't pursue a goal 'cause you think it's expected,
As your emotional well-being can be negatively affected.
Don't try to attain goals, just because they're in fashion.
Make your heart sing! Follow your passion!
Seize a dream that will make you happy and proud,
Make the most of your life, don't play for the crowd.
'Cause in life there are few greater sins,
Than ignoring the dreams you've repressed deep within.

—KL

IDENTIFYING CRITICAL WANTS AND NEEDS

Understanding that your goals are to make life choices that reflect what you truly desire in your life and the person you most want to be, you must take all of the focused time necessary to **identify your critical wants and needs:**

- What you most dearly want and value

- What you absolutely do not want in and for your life

- What you need in order to be happy, fulfilled, and at peace

- What kind of person you truly aspire to be

During your mining explorations, you can ask yourself some of the following **clarifying questions** that may help you to clarify and home in on what you truly want in and for your life:

- What do I deeply want in my life?

- Who do I specifically want in my life?

- What kinds of people do I want in my life?

- What do I most want to accomplish in the short term?

- What do I most want to accomplish in the long run?

- What kind of person would I ideally like to be?

- If there were no restrictions or impediments, what would I do in and with my life?

- What do I want to change about myself or improve upon?

- What do I love about myself and want to safeguard?

- What do I cherish above all else?

- What are the gifts, talents, and accomplishments of others that I would like to emulate?

- If I could have three wishes in my life, what would they be?

- What truly moves me?

- What brings me the greatest, deepest happiness?

- What brings me, or would bring me, the deepest lasting peace and contentment?

- What would my ideal life be like?

VISUAL REPRESENTATION OF GOLD-AND-TRUTH PRIORITIZATION

ist-making can serve as a visual establishment and reminder of your priorities. After you have carefully considered the questions in the previous chapter, as practice, try making three *Lists**:

- The first *List* should include the things that you most dearly want in and for your life. Write down what will make your heart sing. This *List* can be titled your *"Aspirational Gold List."*

- The second *List* should be composed of the things, thoughts, kinds of people, values, and the like that you do not want in your life. This is your *"Toxic Gold List."*

- The third *List* should contain the aspirational personal qualities that you want to incorporate into your behavioral repertoire as you seek to be the best person you're capable of

---

* These *Lists* along with others can be found in the Appendix at the back of this book. You can also download these and other key *Lists* online at positivelifechoicepsychology.com in the *Aspire Higher* section.

being, live your greatest life, and fulfill your highest potentials. This *List* can include the most admirable qualities of others that you would like to emulate. This is your *"Truth List."*

Taking your time to thoughtfully, earnestly, and comprehensively fill out your *Lists* is highly recommended for at least four reasons:

- *List*-making helps you to be a more active, engaged, reflective, and effective participant in this oh-so-important process.

- When you write something down or type it, you can see and absorb it. As a result, the nuggets of "gold" (your thoughts, wants, needs, and aspirations) that you have identified may be much more memorable and helpful, as they will crystalize in your mind what your true aspirations are. Additionally, by making your *Lists*, you will likely feel as though you've accomplished a real, enabling, and empowering first step in your quest to attain your goals and live your truth.

- You can review and, when appropriate, amend your *Lists* in the future so that they accurately reflect your then current, most potent *Gold* and *Truth*.

- This highly active process can help you to dissipate the fear-paralysis that you may experience when trying to move forward with honestly identifying and securing what you truly want in and for your life.

CONSTRUCTING YOUR *LISTS*

Okay! Time to construct your *Lists* and be the most effective Gold and Truth miner possible. Remember, if you can identify your most treasured values, goals, and dreams, and visualize your best self, you will have an easier time making life choices that reflect your vision.

You can make your *Lists* even more effective by putting your most treasured pieces of Gold and Truth—including the things, thoughts, values, and kinds of people you *don't* want in your life—at the very top of your *Lists*. This exercise gives you a visual of the highest goals, values, and aspirations that you want to shoot for and attain.

When you have carefully completed some or all of your *Lists*, check them for "purity," because you always want to be working with the pure truth. One way to do a "purity check" is to ask yourself whether you have been totally honest in your mining and *List* compilation. If you have not been stone-cold real for any reason, the efficacy of the data that you will be working with and basing your life choices on will be compromised, and everything you do thereafter will be similarly compromised and negatively affected. So, purity is paramount!

To this end, here are some questions for which you need to dig down deep to most effectively answer. Nondefensively, and with great courage and pure passion for living your ideal life, ask yourself:

- Do my *Lists* truly reflect who I am and what I most deeply want?

- Is there any reason why (perhaps fear of failure or fear of success) I have not identified my purest values, Gold, and Truth?

- Have I compromised my responses in any way because I'm being influenced by what important and/or influential others want from or expect of me?

If after careful and honest review of your *Lists* you need to amend some of your responses or change the order of some answers to make sure that *the* most preeminent values, goals, and dreams are at the top of your *Lists*, please take the time necessary to make the appropriate changes.

Once you have completed your *Lists*, please read them, absorb them, and remember them. Then, when you make your future life choices, make sure that these choices reflect and are in harmony with your highest goals, most dearly held values and dreams, and your truth. By making life choices that are consistent with your highest values and your truth, you instill into your *Heart-of-Hearts* extremely potent feelings of self-love, high self-esteem, self-worth, and the confidence that you can effect great positive change in your life. And as the airlines advise when you are about to begin a flight, "Please fasten your seat belt first and then fasten others' seat belts that need fastening." By instilling the requisite amount of love into your *Heart-of-Hearts* first, you're much better equipped and far more ready and willing to show and give love to others. All this beautiful fruit will manifest from making the time and effort to identify your highest values, goals, and truth.

I wish you tremendous success and fulfillment in your gold- and truth-mining processes!

HOW TO JUMP-START
YOUR LIFE

You don't have to be shackled to your past, your fears,
or your current life situation. You can break free
with each positive life choice that you make.

—KL

We are all at different places in our lives, and have different backgrounds, challenges, and values. Rabbi David Woznica expressed this thought eloquently when he observed, "We are not in the same boat, just in the same storm in different boats." This diversity is to be treasured. That said, I assume that if you're reading this book, you share with other readers the objectives and values of aspiring to lift the quality of your life, finding love in your heart and in your life, and enjoying a country and world filled with peace, respect, civility, and compassion.

As we touched on earlier, we are going through one of the most difficult times in our history as we are still battling COVID-19 and are plagued with uncertainty, unrest, rancor, racism, pervasive violence, tremendous loss, and heartbreak. In some cases, enormous economic pressures fuel already extreme tensions and angst. We are all suffering in our own, very personal ways. But there IS a bright and beautiful light ahead and much to be optimistic about. Here are your **jump-start steps** to lift your life, along with explanations as to why and how they work.

STEP ONE—RECOGNIZE THE HUGE IMPORTANCE OF THE POSITIVE CHOICE

It is essential that you embrace the core concept that, no matter where you are in your life and how challenging it is, as long as you're alive, you can change the course of and significantly improve your life by the positive choices that you make, by the positive people and things that you will keep in or bring into your life, by elevating yourself and others, and by believing that there is something far better awaiting you if you take these highly beneficial steps.

I recall, years ago, that a tabloid magazine show, *A Current Affair*, apparently was losing viewers at a precipitous rate because of the strong negativity of its day-to-day content. My guess is that the show's producers did some research, which led them to change the tone and content of the show so that it was far more positive. I'll never forget the TV commercials that the production executives ran to let viewers know that they were changing and improving their show, as those commercials depicted a man taking out a big can full of garbage. The tagline of the ad was "We're taking out the trash!" Like that show, you, too, want to take the trash, negativity, fear, and useless clutter out of your mind, your consciousness, your *Heart-of-Hearts*, and your life.

Think of a hot air balloon—sometimes you have to throw expendable things out that are weighing you down in order for the balloon to ascend and reach its greatest heights. It's the same thing with us. We have to discard those negative and toxic things and people who bring us down, in order to attain our greatest heights. So, in your mind, your *Heart-of-Hearts*, and your life, get rid of the negativity, negative self-talk, and your self-defeating mindset, along with the things and people who bring you down, and free yourself to ascend to your greatest heights!

Your love, psychological and physical well-being, and self-image are so worth saving and treasuring, so fill and imbue your *Heart-of-Hearts* and your life with positivity, hope, optimism, love, and your highest values—which are your gold and your truth.

In order to accomplish this goal, you must make conscious choices throughout your day to aspire higher and opt for the positive life choice, rather than default to the sometimes easier road of settling for the negative. If you're figuratively mired in mud, you must rise from whatever low point you are in your life, shower off, get a fresh, clean start, and begin making positive life choices from this moment on. With each positive life choice that you make, be it big or small, you begin to jump-start and rebuild or reshape your life. When you make positive choices, you can dissipate your fears and paralysis, and develop the core confidence that YOU CAN AND WILL master important moments, elevate the quality of your life, and significantly raise your spirits and feelings of mastery. All great, self-enhancing steps and improvements!

I remember competing in a national junior tennis tournament called the Easter Bowl when I was about seventeen. I was playing a top-ranked player from Europe and had lost the first set 0–6 and was losing the second set 1–5. Obviously, things could not have been going worse for me in the match, as I was getting blitzed by my opponent. I'll never forget the moment when, just before I served, I thought, *I'm going to make major changes in my approach and strategy, and instead of hitting my strokes with pace, which my opponent seems to thrive on, I'm going to vary the pace and spin on my strokes and use the short backspace of the court to my advantage. I'm also going to play every stroke of every point as if the match depends on it so I'm hyperfocused on each precious point, as I'm quickly running out of time to make a comeback.* Just before I served, I quietly said to myself, with as much optimism as I could muster, "Okay, Kenny, FROM HERE! LET'S GO!"

That match has ever so vividly stuck in my mind for all of these years, because, stroke by stroke, point by point, and game by game, I came back to win that match, 0–6, 7–6, 6–1, and score a huge, elating upset win. That match was a transformational life lesson for me, as it showed me that I have the power and ability to turn the tide on the tennis court and in life.

I recall a major golf tournament many years ago in which Tiger Woods, during his heyday, was trailing the leader by five strokes going into the final day of play. He wound up winning the tournament by one stroke. When he was interviewed after his victory as to how he managed to come back and win the tournament after trailing by five strokes, he, in essence, confidently said, "I've come back many times before from even worse deficits, so I knew that I could do it again."

Interestingly, ever since the evening that I came back from so far behind in my Easter Bowl match, I've been confident that if I have the right strategies and I make positive choice after positive choice, I can accomplish almost anything that I put my mind to. In this instance, I could clearly relate to what Tiger was saying. The takeaway here is that you never truly know in your *Heart-of-Hearts* that you can accomplish something until you actually do it. You can think and hope that you can do it, but you don't truly know that you can until you do it. The key for you is to begin to take accomplishable baby step after baby step, by making small positive life choices every chance you get. Secure and enjoy your sweet and gratifying choice-making victories. Think of it this way: in the same way I played every stroke in my Easter Bowl match to its fullest, every time you have the chance to make a positive life choice is your golden opportunity to elevate your life, confidence, self-esteem, and self-image.

After you've chosen to make a series of life-enhancing choices, your *Heart-of-Hearts* will begin to be filled with empowering, soul- and spirit-lifting feelings of confidence and mastery. Your penchant to default to the negativity bias should be severely diminished or negated, and you will know that your positive life choices have enhanced your life, your spirit, and your well-being. You will also have the valid, tried-and-true confidence to make many more life-lifting positive choices because you will KNOW that you can, because like Tiger, you've done it many times before.

I suggest that you adopt the following mindset moving forward that digital marketing consultant Ben Francia has gifted us with: when you get up in the morning each day, as well as during your day, tell yourself, "It's a good day to have a GREAT DAY!" And the way to make your day as great as it can be is FROM HERE! RIGHT NOW! LET'S GO! It's time to elevate your game, your spirits, and your life by making positive life choices every opportunity you can.

STEP TWO—IDENTIFY YOUR PETS

> *You always have to find a motivator, something that really moves you, that inspires you to get up from the bed [each morning] and really want to improve and move on with your life . . . On a daily basis you need to have short-term goals . . . that inspire.*[1]
>
> **-NOVAK DJOKOVIC**

Earlier, we discussed the concept of mining and knowing your truth and your gold: your truth is comprised of the things you want the most in and for your life, and your gold is the person you most aspire to be. If you've done an effective and honest job of identifying your gold and truth, you have found huge motivators that will organically lead you to look forward to getting up each morning and living your life to the fullest, elevating your life, and making positive choices in order to attain your gold and live your truth.

Let's now discuss the all-important concept of your "PETS," which are your Personal Emotional Triggers. Your PETS are composed of your gold and your truth, and they are the things, events dreams, aspirations, and goals that strike the deepest chords within your *Heart-of-Hearts* and your psyche. **Effectively identifying, framing, and visualizing your PETS can lead to you breaking the status quo of your poor, deleterious behavior patterns and habits and can also motivate you to do great things for and with your life.** Pretty great, right? Let me share some examples with you.

Years ago, my car had an analog phone, which I placed against my ear for many hours a day as I spoke with clients. After many months of prolonged use of this phone, I began to get headaches after phone calls. Maybe it was just a coincidence, but I was certain that I could feel some force, such as radiation, coming through the receiver on that phone, as my ear felt "funny" each time I used my phone.

One day, an acquaintance, who happened to be an executive at a major phone company that we all know, offhandedly mentioned the tremendous amount of insurance that company had taken out in anticipation of the huge number of people who will possibly contract brain cancer as a result of having cellular conversations by holding their phones up to their ears for extended periods of time.

To say that this individual rocked my world would be a vast understatement. So, the next day, I went to see my doctor about my headaches. After examining me, he said, "Everything looks okay, but I'm going to send you for a brain scan, just to be safe."

I cannot adequately articulate what the thought and the all-too-vivid visual of undergoing brain surgery did to me, but needless to say, it scared the living breath out of me!

A couple of days later I went to the imaging center for my

examination. During the brain-scan procedure, I established a good rapport with the primary technician. After the completion of the procedure, sensing that he could put my fears to rest, the technician said, "I just want you to know, you're okay. But trust me, those analog cell phones can kill you!"

Incredibly relieved and thankful that I was all right, but still shaken from having exposed myself to what seemed to be significant danger, I made a resolution: From that day on, I would NEVER AGAIN have a conversation holding my cell phone against my ear. Instead, I would either use a headset or put my phone on speaker mode—to have as much separation from the alleged radiation as possible.

What I gleaned from this story are the following insights:

- My PETS or my Personal Emotional Triggers in this case were:

  a. My powerful fear of being a patient in a hospital, being treated for a life-threatening condition

  b. My powerful fear of having brain cancer

  c. My not wanting to die

  d. My fervent desire to live a long, healthy, life

These incredibly strong, highly emotionally charged PETS struck the deepest chords within me.

This experience compelled me to break my behavioral pattern of always holding my cell phone to my ear during conversations. This experience and these particular PETS from that day forward motivated me to make the positive life choice to no longer subject myself to the alleged possible cancer-causing radiation of analog or other cell phones. As a result, a beneficial behavioral modification took place.

Here's another PET story:

Throughout my mother's life, she was late for everything: school, work, appointments, her sister's wedding, and even her own wedding. This was her behavioral script and status quo until one day, about seven years into my parents' marriage. On that evening, my mom was unconscionably late for her date with my dad. Their plan on that snowy, blustery cold evening was to have dinner and see a Broadway play. However, as a result of my mother's extreme tardiness, my dad wound up standing outside the restaurant for over two hours, waiting for her and worrying. When she finally arrived, too late to have dinner, my dad was frozen and nearly apoplectic. As they entered the theater, they were told that they had already missed the first twenty minutes of the play. My dad wisely held his anger and said nothing to my mom for the remainder of the evening.

The next day, my father, in a much calmer state, came into my mother's dressing room as she was applying her makeup. "Betty," he began, "I don't know what to say . . . Your behavior is a mystery to me. If you were stupid, then I could understand and I might forgive you. But you're one of the smartest people I know. And generally, I think that you're a really nice person. So, I ask you: How could you let me stand on a street corner for two hours on such a freezing cold night? It's beyond me. I can't begin to tell you how bad it makes me feel and how hurt I am. How can you be so uncaring, so impossibly *mean*? How could you?"

My dad then turned and left the room. My mom was stunned. She had never before thought of herself as inconsiderate. For my mom, "mean" was the key word and her trigger—her PET. Being called "mean" bothered her tremendously. For some time afterward, my mom wondered why she was so disturbed by it. Then it hit her like a ton of bricks. She associated the word with her mother, whom she abhorred! Her mother had hated her since she was born.

Her mother had physically and emotionally abused her through-out her childhood. My mom perceived her mother as the "Queen of MEAN," and that's why the word struck such a primal chord deep in her psyche. In no way would my mom ever want to be like her mother. That was it. That's why she was so upset. Then my mom had another breakthrough: She had tried to emulate her loving dad in every way possible, and her dad was *always* late.

Appearing to be "mean," with all of its horribly negative associa-tions and connotations, was the PET that shattered my mom's toxic behavioral scripting. She never wanted to be like the mother she detested. So, on that day, she made the conscious life choice to never be late again, and, in almost every instance thereafter, not only was my mom not late, but she often arrived early.

My mom said that she accomplished this extremely positive behav-ioral change by thinking about being (perceived as) "mean" each time that she had an appointment. The super-high-voltage charges of the PET motivated and catalyzed her to get ready for her engagements in a timely fashion so that she would always be on time.

When explaining all of this to me, my mom shared that early in the day, whenever she had an engagement, she would frame the fol-lowing question: "Do I want to be late for my appointment and once again be perceived as mean, because I'm acting just like my mother whom I abhor, or do I want to be considerate and respectful of others' time?" When she framed her options in this manner, my mom always made the constructive choice to arrive for her dates on time or early. Effectively framing the choice before her aided her by strongly rein-forcing the fact that she wanted to never be like her mom.

To review: My mom's newfound ability to clearly see and act consistently with her gold (not to be perceived as "mean") and her truth (to be a kind and thoughtful person) became a reality after my dad triggered a huge emotional reaction within her, compelling her to break her highly toxic pattern of behavior. The key here is that my dad's words to my mom were so highly emotionally charged that they overpowered the compulsion that led her to always be late. Please note the four processes at play here:

- My mom identified/recognized that her PET was that she abhorred being called and perceived as MEAN.

- She thereafter consciously chose to use this highly charged PET to self-motivate her to strive to never be late again. For my mother, the PET of not being MEAN acted like super-charged dynamite in blowing up a figurative railroad track of deeply embedded, destructive behavioral choices.

- Effectively framing the choice before her motivated my mother even more to make the positive life choice of being punctual.

- As a direct result, my mother's self-sabotaging behavioral pattern in this area was broken and conquered, and the beneficial life choice to consistently arrive for her appointments on time and not keep people waiting (interminably) was the beautiful result. A highly positive piece of behavioral modification took place.

To take this example a bit further, the highly potent PET of my mom not wanting to be the abominable parent that she perceived her mother to be led her to make the conscious choice each and every day of her life to be the direct opposite of her mom in raising me; my mom was loving, kind, nonjudgmental, and supportive.

Now, let's focus on the important process of artfully framing the life choice before you so that you're inevitably led to make a positive life choice whenever the opportunity arises. As I mentioned earlier, I am someone who *hates* the thought of being a patient in a hospital. I will do anything and change any behavior to avoid being operated on for an illness or a serious health-related problem. This visualization scares me to death! This profound fear is one of my most potent, energy-charged PETS. I also cherish my health and general well-being above almost anything else, along with that of my family and loved ones. I developed this health-focused mindset from my dad, who always took excellent care of himself, ate sensibly, and got lots of exercise and rest. The combination of these highly constructive behaviors and his sturdy genetic endowment enabled my dad to live a healthy and vital life until he passed away at the age of one hundred years and two months.

I, as an admiring son and fan, have wanted to do everything that I can to replicate my dad's wonderful health and extraordinary long and active life. When I was younger, one obstacle for me was that I truly loved fried foods, and they were a regular part of my daily diet until the day that I visited "Ben," a family friend who was in the hospital. Ben was in his late fifties and was about to have his second major bypass surgery after suffering a second heart attack. He was obviously scared to death that he might not survive the operation and never again be with his loving wife, his beautiful children, and his adoring mother. Seeing this man cooped up and scared to death in his hospital room absolutely terrified me. When the nurses came to wheel Ben into surgery, my heart beat faster and faster, and tears flooded my eyes and rolled down my cheeks. I so felt for him and his family.

Ben's wife whispered to me as he left the room, "Ben has severely clogged arteries, and he never watched what he ate. He thought that he was indestructible." I couldn't help but take note that she spoke of him in the past tense. Her eyes welled up with tears. I will never forget the scene of Ben's wife and mother doing everything they could to appear optimistic and uplifting when talking to Ben just before he was sedated, and then leaving the room after he drifted off to sleep, breaking down with inconsolable tears, wondering if they would ever see him alive again.

Soon after Ben went to surgery, I left the room. After saying goodbye to everyone, I immediately framed the pressing issue before me: Do I want the momentary pleasure of the taste of the fried foods and thereby seriously risk ending up like Ben? Do I want to be held captive, cooped up, and *totally vulnerable*—in a hospital? Do I want to be absolutely scared to death as I await a potentially life-ending surgery? And do I want to keep eating fried foods and potentially irreparably damage my heart so that I seriously risk not enjoying the long, vital, active life I crave? Or, do I say an emphatic "NO, THANK YOU!" to fried foods from now on, and hopefully never face heart or any other related surgery?

I then visualized myself in a hospital bed like Ben, awaiting surgery, scared beyond belief that I would never see my loved ones again. I also visualized the deep pain and angst that I would put my loved ones through should I need to undergo such surgery or die during or soon after surgery simply because I wasn't disciplined enough to refrain from eating fried foods.

The collective energy charges from my frame and visualizations were so extraordinarily powerful that they totally negated any allure that I might have regarding the good taste and momentary pleasure that I might derive from eating fried foods. As a result, at *Crunch Time!*, whenever I'm faced with eating a fried food, I tap into the above-mentioned PETS, and I'm then able to value clearly and resolutely. I'm thrilled to say that the number of fingers on one hand represent the number of times over the past thirty-five years that I have eaten something fried.

Your three takeaways here are: 1) certain PETS evoke supremely strong energy charges within you, 2) your goal is to identify or create your PETS, and by effectively framing and visualizing these super-motivators, you are able to adopt or change almost any behavior, and 3) by skillfully using impactful frames and visualizations, you can push your own emotional buttons, thereby motivating and empowering yourself to make choices that reflect your most treasured gold and truth.

To reinforce the concept of consciously choosing to push your own emotional buttons in order to achieve a highly positive result, let's recall the story about how Tom Brady allegedly used his feelings of being disrespected, hurt, and angered over not being chosen until the 199th pick in the 2000 NFL draft—his PET—to motivate himself every time he took the field to be the best quarterback in history. Brady's is a wonderful example of how someone can skillfully push their own emotional buttons to reach incredible heights and success.

What we can glean from these stories is that your gold and your truth are the things you want the most in and for your life, and the person you most aspire to be or become, respectively. When going through the process of lifting your life by making positive life choices, your goal is to identify the things, events, people, and values that you most want in and for your life; the things you love or very much enjoy doing; as well as the things, people, events, and values that you abhor, loathe, and hate. All of these pieces of gold and truth are your supercharged PETS that can motivate you to time after time make positive life choices that will put your life on a healthy, constructive, success-evoking, fulfilling, and soul-nourishing track.

STEP THREE—MAKE A LIFE-ELEVATING CHOICE

Supremely motivated by your PETS and your strong desire to substantially raise the quality of your choices, your life, and your confidence to effect major beneficial change in your life—**make a**

positive, life-lifting choice! If you make a life choice that also positively impacts and elevates others, you exponentially increase the positive feelings that are instilled in your *Heart-of-Hearts*. Think of it as you scoring significant *Heart-of-Hearts* superbonus points! We will discuss this concept more in the "Solutionary" chapter in Part 4 of this book.

STEP FOUR—ACKNOWLEDGE AND SAVOR YOUR GOOD DECISION

Whenever you make a choice that you're happy with and are proud of, acknowledge it, enjoy it, and savor it. This way, the great feelings of a choice well-made and the knowledge that you consciously took positive ownership of your emotions and your choices will fill your *Heart-of-Hearts*. This will result in you developing the unshakable core confidence that you've made great life choices before and you can do it again—just like Tiger.

REVIEW THE STEPS

Step One is to strive to put positive thoughts, people, and events in your life and to commit to making positive life choices in connection with each precious opportunity that comes your way. Please remember, trains go where the tracks take them; similarly, the track or path of your life and your ability to effect positive and beneficial life change rest in YOUR hands, with the life choices that you make.

Step Two is to identify your strongest motivators—your supercharged PETS—that will lead you to make highly beneficial life changes and positive life choices.

Step Three is to make a positive life choice that reflects your gold and your truth—your preeminent values and goals.

Step Four is to acknowledge and savor life choices well-made so that highly potent, empowering feelings of accomplishment are instilled in your *Heart-of-Hearts*. In turn, these feelings will give you the confidence and the motivation to make more positive behavioral changes and life choices in the future.

"PET" CARE

One other strategy I want to share with you involves your "PET" care, which for us means that you continually check the potency of your PETS. Throughout your life, continue to identify your gold and truth, but also ask yourself, "Has the passage of time or the acquisition of some new information or insight made a certain goal more or less important to me, which will thereby affect its potency?"

The valuation of your current emotion-generated energy charges is of crucial import because, as we have discussed, the more you value your gold, the higher its energy charge is for you. Another reason why you want to continually check the potency of your PETS is that this process empowers you to *sustain* your life choice–making success.

Here's an illustration: A few years ago, I was contacted by one of this country's most well-known weight-loss companies. An executive from that company explained to me that in the great majority of cases, when an individual signs up with the company to lose weight, the client does so because, in essence, some specific person or event (or potential event) in that client's life is triggering this decision.

This catalyzing event might be a New Year's resolution; a new love interest; the spring/summer bikini/swimsuit season's impending arrival; an upcoming wedding or other important event; a new job; or an approaching vacation (the motivating event or PET). This executive then shared the profound problem for his company: "In the new year, we get a slew of new signups, but then the drop-off rate after four or five weeks is tremendous." He continued, "The individuals who become members are *initially* motivated, for whatever their reason is to begin losing weight, but when they lose that initial motivation—which often happens very quickly—we never hear from them again. There's no staying power!" This executive sought my counsel and help in connection with how his company could enable its clients to sustain their motivation over time to want to lose weight.

Although I didn't move forward with that company, my analysis regarding this huge dropout problem is that everyone who makes the life choice to sign up and begin dieting so that he or she can lose weight, does so because the energy charge(s) generated from a certain piece or pieces of their gold (e.g., a New Year's resolution, wanting to fit into a bikini or swimsuit because of an upcoming vacation or because spring/summer is coming, or due to a new love interest or an impending job interview) are highly potent, but once their initial motivation diminishes or goes away, they leave the program. So, the key is to find other pieces of gold or new motivators to supplement or replace the original one(s) in order to keep the enthusiasm high enough that these individuals want to continue to stay with the program, lose weight, and keep it off.

An example of changing out your PETS in order to keep you supremely motivated to make positive choices and attain your most treasured goals is as follows: Originally, I identified certain PETS to motivate me to lose weight, keep me healthy, and be in the very best shape to play my best tennis. But with time, my motivations changed. Now that I'm a loving husband and dad, my strongest motivators are the happiness and well-being of my wife and children. So I will do almost anything it takes to enhance their lives and be healthy and vital for them for as many years as I'm blessed to live.

REVIEWING THE PET PROCESS

There are two insights to take away here:

- When you make a life choice to do something that will lift your life, such as committing to continually make positive life choices, lose weight, stop drinking, smoking, or losing your temper, you are initially fueled by your strongest energy charges generated by the gold and truth that comprise your PETS.

- If you desire to enjoy SUSTAINED success in this endeavor, you must be committed to regularly checking the potency of your PETS, as well as identifying new motivators so that you can replace the PETS whose energy charge potency has diminished over time with ones that are more highly charged. Thus, if one of your initial motivators loses its juice, your goal is to find one or more other high-potency PETS to take their place. This way you keep your energy charges, motivation, frames, and visualizations supercharged and at maximum effectiveness. You do this because you want to attain SUSTAINED success, fulfillment, and happiness. No fifteen minutes of fame or one-hit wonders for us!

Part 4

The *PLCP* Philosophies, Aspirations, Ideals, and Words That Will Fill Your *Heart-of-Hearts* with Love

In this part of our book, we focus on *The Positive Life Choice Psychology Lifestyle Philosophies* that will fill your *Heart-of-Hearts* with empowering feelings of high self-esteem and self-worth, as well as invaluable self-love that, in turn, will catalyze you to treasure yourself and your well-being; to aspire higher; to listen to, understand, respect, have compassion and empathy for others; and to love unconditionally. And if you have experienced hurt, pain, rejection, anger, rage, and other feelings that have hardened your *Heart-of-Hearts*, following the *PLCP* Philosophies over time will dissipate and dissolve the embedded hard feelings of hurt, rejection, and anger that are lodged within you. Through this highly salutary transformation process, you will fill and refill your *Heart-of-Hearts* with positive, loving, highly constructive thoughts, ideals, and scripts for behavior, all of which will motivate and inspire you to do great and beneficial things for yourself, for those you love, and for those around you.

Once again, your goal throughout your life is to continually instill as much positivity, love, caring, compassion, empathy, and the like into your *Heart-of-Hearts*. Constructive, loving choices and actions toward yourself and others will be the sweet results. The concepts and magical words discussed in the chapters that follow will be some of your most effective and potent ways to lovingly fill your *Heart-of-Hearts*. Let's dream with passion and commitment and aspire higher. Please open your *Heart-of-Hearts* and your mind and enjoy!

EYESIGHT ISN'T
NECESSARILY INSIGHT

True understanding, respect, and
appreciation of others illuminate
the path to unite us all.

—KL

John Lennon & Paul McCartney put it best when, in their hit song "Strawberry Fields," they sang about how it is easy to live with your eyes closed, not seeing or understanding the reality around us.

One of the most common means by which we navigate the challenges of everyday life is through generalizing, categorizing, compartmentalizing, and profiling. These processes enable us to quickly make what we often believe are "survival-based" judgments that rely on instincts of self-preservation. For example, is this person safe to be around or potentially dangerous? Are they like us or very different than we are? Are they warm and friendly or cold and aloof?

AVOIDING SNAPSHOT JUDGMENTS

Because we live in a fast-paced world where immediate gratification is often the end goal, we want answers and insights instantly so that we can make our snap judgments and quickly move on. But eyesight isn't necessarily insight. In order to aspire higher and be the wisest person we're capable of, we need to take the time to understand where a person has been and who that person is in order to truly know what they are about and why they perceive and act as they do. Essentially, you want to take time to study an exploratory X-ray rather than quickly gloss over a snapshot.

Taking the time and making the effort to respectfully glean true understanding of someone is in many ways similar to studying the "legislative history" of a law. That is, the modification and edification processes that a proposed law goes through in the Senate and House of Representatives before it's finally passed. From understanding the legislative history of a law, we can ascertain the "why," the "what," and the "how" of a law. In essence, we learn *how* to correctly interpret the law by understanding *why* the law was originally introduced and ultimately passed; *why* it is drafted as it is; *what* the law is supposed to accomplish; and *how* the law is intended to be administered. So, knowing the legislative history of a law enables us to understand it, in essence, by understanding where it's coming from. We may not always initially agree with a law, but if we do a little more research and thereby glean knowledge and understanding, we may completely change our mind about the law and even embrace it.

It's the same thing with people. If you understand where they're coming from—their personal histories and experiences, values, opinions, likes, and dislikes—you may well interpret what you are seeing or hearing more accurately and objectively, and thus be a far more effective, compassionate, and humane decision-maker regarding those individuals, their actions, and their needs. Additionally, attaining true understanding of others can break down seemingly impenetrable walls and defenses, and lead to sincere, mutual appreciation and respect, as well as fulfilling collaborations.

PERSONAL BIAS

On the other side of the coin, we, too, bring our own unique perceptions, views, experiences, behavioral scripts, insecurities, and defenses to the table when we view events, things, and people. Knowing this, you want to aspire higher, by thoughtfully and insightfully considering your background when making your assessments and choices. You also want to make sure that others are clear regarding your background, so that they too can be more understanding of, empathic regarding, and receptive to your ideas, suggestions, or requests. How we appear and how much we share about ourselves with others gives them the opportunity to see and understand who we are and why we think and value as we do.

A memorable story illustrating that eyesight isn't necessarily insight involves a client of mine, "Claire Wilson." One day, Claire entered a wedding reception that was already underway. She headed directly to her seat at table 28 and didn't stop to make eye contact with anyone. While I was standing at the buffet table, I heard three different takes on Claire's entrance. One woman said, "Look at Claire Wilson. She thinks she's better than all of us. The 'princess' just walks in and glides to her table. She didn't even smile at those she passed. *Boy, is she cold and stuck-up!*" A second woman remarked, "There's Claire. God, she's so beautiful, but she doesn't even know it. *She's so shy*. If I don't go over to her and introduce her to people, she'll never have the confidence to do it herself." While a guy standing nearby shared, "Did you see Claire walk in here? *She's doing everything she can to avoid me.* I don't know what I did to make her angry."

As it turned out, Claire's best friend had been in a car accident the day before, and Claire's thoughts as she entered the reception were all about her friend. *Will she live? If she does, will she be paralyzed?* In honor of her cousin's marriage, Claire made an appearance at the wedding, left quickly, and then rejoined her friend at the hospital.

The manner in which Claire entered the reception was interpreted three different ways by three different individuals. All of them brought their own personal set of experiences, values, perceptions, insecurities and defenses, needs, and more to the interpretation. As a result, Claire was thought to be "snobby," "shy," and "angry." That day, she was none of those things. She was preoccupied.

SEEING PAST OUR BIASES

I would now like to elaborate on my own personal story. As I mentioned, as a youngster, I was overweight, awkward, clumsy, insecure, and an overall late bloomer. The good news for me was that my mom took the time to understand me and my needs. She was able to correctly intuit that I needed to be athletic as a means to feel better about myself physically and to bond with my athletic dad, who at that point seemed to work all the time, except on Sundays. When I took up POP Tennis, a form of short-court tennis, I found that because the court was relatively small, the net low, the bounce of the punctured ball lower than that of a traditional tennis ball, and the face of the short racquet close to my hand, I was able to be successful at a sport for the first time in my life. I can tell you that the empowering feelings of mastery and accomplishment were amazing and intoxicating. I loved being good at something—especially because I gained my dad's approval and respect. I poured my energies and focus into POP Tennis, with great results. I also lost weight and became far more agile.

During the summer between seventh and eighth grade, I began to play tennis at summer camp, and because I was so adept at POP Tennis, the transition was easy. So, because of my tangible success playing both POP Tennis and tennis, I gained confidence and valid feelings of self-worth. My focus as a student, however, left much to be desired, because I couldn't have cared less about my schoolwork. Thank goodness I had a good memory, so I tested well enough, and because my mom understood me, she cut me lots (and lots) of slack, as I rarely did my homework.

When I was fortunate enough to be accepted to Brooklyn Polytechnic Preparatory Country Day School, aka "Poly Prep," I found myself in a college preparatory school among many smart and highly driven students. A few weeks after enrollment, I went out for the varsity tennis team and told the coach about all of my POP Tennis successes. I must have been convincing because he arranged a challenge match between me and the returning varsity #1 player, who was a senior. I won the match 6–1, 6–0, and from that day forward, I was the number one player on the varsity team as a freshman.

That was the good news. The not-so-great news was that this early athletic success and highly favorable school publicity as "The Freshman Phenom" further reinforced in my psyche that being great at a racquet sport was my ticket to all sorts of addicting and intoxicating positive reinforcement, and that academics weren't as important—thus my work habits and grades reflected my half-hearted commitment to schoolwork. (Actually, one-tenth-hearted would be more accurate.) The result of this huge imbalance was that our assistant headmaster, "Mr. Smith," simply perceived me as a not-too-bright jock, and for the first two-and-a-half years at Poly, I gave him no reason to think otherwise.

Every spring, Poly held its end-of-the-school-year academic and awards ceremony. It was quite the gathering—parents, family, and alumni. In each of my first three years, I was given the "Most Valuable Tennis Player" award. In all three years, the same Poly/Harvard alumnus, "Mr. Christopher," gave out the "Harvard Award" to the most academically accomplished member of the senior class. At the conclusion of the awards ceremony during my junior year, Mr. Christopher approached me and said, "Ken, I've seen you receive the tennis award each of the past three years. Have you ever considered going to Harvard?" Before I could answer, Mr. Smith (who was a proud Harvard alumnus) took me by the shoulders and directed me away, telling Mr. Christopher, "He's NOT Harvard material." Mr. Smith then introduced Mr. Christopher to the class members who he felt were "Harvard material."

I heard Mr. Smith's remark, and feelings of hurt and shame surged through me like a bolt of lightning. Upon reflection, the saving grace of that day was that I never considered applying to Harvard, as I too didn't think that I was "Harvard material."

The problem with Mr. Smith's perception of me as some dumb jock was that he was the gatekeeper for all college admissions recommendations. In my junior year, I learned what I was in for during my college application class, as he in all seriousness suggested that I apply to lower-level colleges and major in underwater basket weaving. Nice!

But when I took a sociology class taught by a wonderful educator, Mr. Morrison, I transformed into an inspired student. The material in that course was game- and life-changing for me. I discovered that I loved the study of people and I was excited and inspired because, for the first time, a teacher of mine looked beyond my "jock" reputation and persona and recognized that I had great passion and potential as a student of sociology.

In the meantime, during my senior year, many schools recruited me. I realized that attending No-Hope State and majoring in basket weaving and pottery making didn't have to be in my imminent future. In fact, three Ivy League universities expressed interest in me. Then a close tennis friend of mine, Richard Scheer, who was a Harvard alumnus and a quasi-recruiter for them, suggested the unfathomable: that I should apply to Harvard. One of the first things that came to mind was that if I had to approach Mr. Smith for a recommendation to his alma mater, he'd either kill me or himself. But after giving the idea some thought, I summoned my courage and asked for a meeting. When I explained that I would be applying to three Ivy League colleges, and mentioned Columbia University and the University of Pennsylvania, his immediate reaction was "You'll *never* be accepted there." When I brought up Harvard, his face turned bright red, and he became apoplectic. As he tried to regain some semblance of composure, he said, all-knowingly, "Don't waste Harvard's time and your money. You'll *never* get in! Besides, I won't even write you the recommendation that you'll need to have your application considered." He then took me by the shoulders and escorted me out of his office. Once again, as he did at the awards ceremony when Mr. Christopher wanted to chat with me about applying to Harvard, Mr. Smith gave me the bum's rush.

That evening, I told my mom about my meeting with Mr. Smith. After giving it a good deal of thought, the next morning, she scheduled a meeting with Mr. Smith. During the meeting, my mom presented Mr. Smith with a photograph of me as an overweight and awkward child. She explained that athletics had helped me to develop both physically and psychologically and had added greatly to my self-confidence and positive outer and inner sense of identity. She told him how POP Tennis and traditional tennis had in fact become an integral part of my life and were almost like crutches that I would need to be weaned from. My mom believed—and effectively conveyed to Mr. Smith—that I was clearly growing and expanding academically. She cited the As that I was getting in my sociology/psychology class, as well as the excellent grades that I was now earning in my other classes. She told Mr. Smith that I had always been a late bloomer and that I was just starting to bloom academically. Somehow my mom got through to him.

After confirming my mom's assertions with my various instructors, Mr. Smith agreed that if my grades continued to rise during that first semester of my senior year, he would write "some kind" of recommendation to Harvard for me—but to be sure, it would *not* be a good one. As the meeting ended, my mom thanked him for his courtesy and for keeping an open mind.

That evening, my mom explained the deal that she had made with Mr. Smith. Because of the confidence and strong feelings of mastery that I was gaining academically, I enjoyed keeping my end of the bargain. That semester, my grades rose substantially, and at the appropriate time, I handed Mr. Smith my Harvard recommendation form, and I was told that he would keep his end of the bargain—by writing a recommendation to Harvard for me—although it wouldn't be an overly positive one.

On April 14, one day before everyone received their college admissions letters of acceptance, I received a call from a wonderful Ivy League university. I had been accepted! I was happy and relieved, but my heart was with Harvard.

The next day, the two top students at Poly were accepted to Harvard. However, the number three student, who was the editor of our newspaper and who had worked his whole high school career for a Harvard admission, was rejected. (Thankfully, he was accepted at Yale.)

That morning, all I could think about was Harvard. I felt that many others unquestionably deserved to go there more than I did, but I knew that if given the chance, I would make the very most of it and appreciate it forever. At ten thirty, an assistant from the front office came into my math class and handed me a note to call home. I knew this was it. My heart pounded. My hands shook. I was short of breath. I had no right to expect a yes, but I wanted it more than anything in my life. I dialed the number. After the phone rang twice, my mom picked up. Laughing with happiness, she said, "You got in! You got into Harvard!"

For a moment or so, I had found nirvana. I jumped up and yelled, "Yes!" attracting the attention of everyone in the front office. Chills ran through me. I asked my mother to read the acceptance letter to me . . . three times. I thanked her for being the best mother ever! I didn't have the language for expressing it back then, but clearly my mom was doing her best in filling my *Heart-of-Hearts* with feelings of self-worth. Since my father was in Europe on business, she was going to call him and send him a telegram. It was a moment that I will never, ever forget.

I knew that my next move was to see Mr. Smith. April 15 was always a big day for Poly, and Mr. Smith was kept abreast of who did and didn't get accepted into which colleges. He already knew through the grapevine that out of the top ten students in our class, only two had been accepted at Harvard. He had been told that I'd been accepted to two Ivy League universities the day before. As I was escorted into Mr. Smith's office, I was doing all that I could to contain my smile and exuberance. Inside, though, I was *bursting*.

He took one look at me and his eyes widened. He realized that his greatest fear had come to pass. I had been accepted to *his* alma mater. He began to stutter as he inquired, "Y-Y-You got in?" I smiled warmly and acted as calmly and gratefully as I could as I told him the good news. He looked down to the floor, and for a moment he was at a loss for words.

I understood how he felt. From his vantage point, others deserved to be accepted far more than I did—if academic accomplishment over the course of a high school career was the sole admissions criterion. In order to fill the gap of silence, I said, "Mr. Smith, I know that others may deserve to be accepted to Harvard more than I do, but I won't let you or Poly down. I do appreciate your keeping an open mind about writing my recommendation to Harvard."

He then said, in as optimistic a tone as he could muster, "I think that you'll be all right. Just remember, you have been given a special opportunity that thousands upon thousands of young people your age dream about. Use it wisely."

As he shook my hand, I responded, "Thank you, sir. I will."

During my first year at Harvard, I made the freshman Dean's List and, just as I did during my career at Poly, I defeated the number one player on the varsity tennis team in a practice match within a few days of my arrival there. After the school year ended, I returned to Brooklyn, and I called Mr. Smith to set up an appointment to see him. At that meeting, I shared the good news with him about my academic achievements. He was happy, and we began to bond, as he realized that what my mom had told him a year or so earlier had been true. Three years later, I called Mr. Smith to tell him that I was going to graduate Harvard magna cum laude. I also shared my tennis successes with him. He told me that my call was fortuitous, because Mr. Christopher, who had given out the Harvard Cup for eight years in a row at our spring semester awards ceremony, had just called to say that he couldn't make it that year. Amazingly, Mr. Smith said, "Kenny, I can't think of anyone more suited than you to give out the Harvard Cup this year." Upon hearing this, my insides swelled up with the kind of love, gratitude, and validation that can't be put into words. My *Heart-of-Hearts* was brimming! Needless to say, I felt great about his offer and accepted his invitation.

Coincidentally, after the awards ceremony concluded, Mr. Smith and I stood in the exact place where Mr. Christopher and I had stood five years earlier, when Mr. Smith took me by the shoulders and escorted me away, saying that I wasn't "Harvard material." Mr. Smith then took me aside and said, "Kenny, even though I'm going to retire this year, one is never too old to learn. You and your mom taught me a great lesson: never prejudge anyone. I thought I knew you—but I didn't. I thought I saw who you were, BUT

EYESIGHT DOESN'T MEAN INSIGHT. I never thought that you were capable of doing as well as you have. From this experience, I've learned to keep an open mind and to see beyond what's apparent. You should thank your mother, because were it not for her faith in you and her great understanding of you, I would never have written any recommendation for you. She's very special." I thanked Mr. Smith and told him that I knew that my mom "is great!"

As he spoke, tears welled up in my eyes. At the end of our meeting, we exchanged the warmest of smiles, a hug, and a long handshake. It was a meeting and a lesson that I will never forget. To this day, I do my best to aspire higher by taking the time to understand and respect where others are coming from and what leads them to act, think, and value as they do. I also strive to never prejudge someone, as "Eyesight isn't necessarily insight." Here's to us all being astutely insightful!

LOOKING BEYOND FACE VALUE

Because individuals can and do see identical matters in such radically diverse ways, these subjective realities can have a material impact upon how you and others perceive issues and the behavioral scripts that are adopted. It's your goal to look deeper and not just accept people at face value—and it is especially important not to prejudge people based on others' subjective opinions and impressions. Hopefully, with deep exploration and understanding, you can act appropriately and in the most enlightened, evolved, and humane manner, as you aspire higher.

We each must make an authentic effort to understand the reasons why relevant others act as they do and try to understand their histories, as this can go a long way in dissipating the potency of the potentially poisonous energy charges that you're dealing with when making a life choice. Here's why: With knowledge of others comes understanding of them, and with understanding comes appreciation and/or identification and respect for where they're coming from and how they see things, which can lead to feeling compassion, sympathy, and empathy for others. In time, these feelings can lead to forgiveness; and once you feel compassion and truly forgive, you can then feel love and a strong desire to do the right thing regarding your choices involving them.

This beautiful evolutionary process will trigger a dissipation of potentially toxic energy charges within your *Heart-of-Hearts* so that you are free to make cognitively clear decisions and choices that reflect your most treasured values and your highest self. It will also melt any hard feelings within you for the person and issue at hand. By truly understanding, respecting, and having compassion for others, and making choices and acting in accordance with this knowledge and these feelings, you will continually fill your *Heart-of-Hearts* with feelings of positive accomplishment, high self-esteem, self-worth, and the like. Expressing love through your choices and actions will instill love within you, and this love will catalyze you to make more compassionate, highest-value choices moving forward, because they make you feel great about yourself and your ability to effect positive change by doing beneficial things for others.

I know that you've heard the saying "It's better to give than receive." For our purposes, by giving and showing love, respect, compassion, and empathy, you will receive one of the most valuable gifts possible—empowering, highly motivating self-love. A true WIN-WIN result! To truly take this path to its fullest, we have to remember to see others for the complex, wonderful beings that they are. I would like, therefore, to close this chapter with the following poem of mine:

LIFE IS LIKE A RORSCHACH TEST

Life is like a Rorschach test,
So, don't be sure your "take's" the best.
As there are different points of view,
And others' "takes" might be right, too.

When anticipating how one might act,
Never forget the crucial fact,
That everyone is a unique case,
And coming from a different place!

People have grown up with different perspectives,
Values, beliefs, and personal objectives.
Because of this, they may fail to see,
What appears—to you—is so obviously
The only correct course of action,
And the one which holds the most attraction.

Keep an open mind and thereby clear the way,
To truly hear what others have to say,
And honestly try to ascertain,
Whether from their ideas you can gain,
A fuller, richer, broader perspective,
And one which isn't so subjective.

When interacting with others—we must try,
To view things through another's eyes,
True objectivity will be your quest,
Remembering life's like a Rorschach test.

—KL

NAMASTE

"Namaste" is a Sanskrit phrase that means "I bow to you." Isabelle Marsh, MSW, writes, "Namaste directly translates to 'the divine in me bows to the divine in you.'"[1] For *The PLCP Lifestyle*, the term "namaste" is fused with all sorts of beautiful meaning. For us, we also take it to mean that "the light and love in me sees, recognizes, appreciates, and honors the light and love in you." Its gentle implications can be interpreted as intending that we see others through eyes of respect, appreciation, understanding, compassion, empathy, caring, and love. It's treating and honoring all others as you want them to treat and honor you.

If defined this way, the term "namaste" gives us the golden path to peace between people; peace and respect between groups, factions, races; peace among nations; and ultimately, world peace.

With the personal and global payoff so meaningful, beneficial, and significant, why not passionately instill this beautiful concept into your *Heart-of-Hearts* and incorporate it into your everyday life—starting now.

Namaste. The light and love in me sees the radiant light and love in you.

THE IMPORTANCE OF MAKING CONSTRUCTIVE LIFE CHOICES

I can't predict the future. If I'm to aspire higher,
my goals are to be open to, accepting of,
and to act constructively regarding the
uncertainty of future events.

—KL

We've all heard the cliché "When you're handed lemons, make lemonade." Let me share some personal lemonade-making stories and recipes with you to illustrate what being constructive means, how it can give you the empowering feelings of confidence and mastery to beneficially change your life's path, and how, by being creatively constructive, you can fill your *Heart-of-Hearts* with these wonderful feelings.

PERSONAL AND CAREER CHOICES

When I was a junior in college, I had the wonderful opportunity to represent the United States in tennis at the Maccabiah Games in Israel. I was honored and thrilled to be chosen and very much looked forward to the opportunity. The one drawback of going to Israel at that time was that the games took place during my study weeks prior to my midyear final exams. As a result, between practicing and competing, I would have put myself in a precarious position with regard to having enough time to prepare for my finals.

As it turned out, a week before I was supposed to leave for Israel, I was diagnosed with mononucleosis. When my blood tests came back, my doctor had me take a physical exam during which he discovered that I had an enlarged spleen, which meant that there was no chance that I could fly on a plane. In fact, he said that I would be bedridden for at least three weeks. Upon hearing this, I was exceedingly disappointed and distraught, as I perceived that this would be my only chance to compete in the Maccabiah Games. (As it turned out, my assessment was correct.)

After digesting the seemingly horrible news for a day or so, I decided to dust myself and my spirits off from the body-blow that I had just suffered. I then thought, *What is the most constructive and best plan of action moving forward, given the disappointing situation at hand?* The answer was easy: I would make the most of my time by studying for finals and writing what I thought could be a breakthrough thesis on the sociological selection of jurors, based upon the sociology, linguistics, and anthropology courses that I had taken the past year and a half. With nothing better to do, I poured myself into the endeavors at hand.

I have always been a believer that events happen for a reason. In this case, I believed that the reason I didn't go to Israel and spend most of my time preparing for and competing in the Maccabiah

Games in lieu of studying was because I was meant to focus on my schoolwork at this pivotal point in my college career. That fortuitous change of focus led to my getting top grades that semester and writing an honors thesis that was awarded the grade of magna cum laude. And I was right—my thesis was regarded by many as a breakthrough work in the field of juror selection.

There is no question in my mind that I never would have received the grades I did or written my honors thesis in the in-depth manner that I had the time to do, had I gone to Israel for two and a half weeks. The thesis that I wrote led me to go to law school, and graduating magna cum laude certainly resulted in Cornell accepting me into their joint law and business program.

Seemingly being given lemons and making lemonade in this situation was a great life lesson for me. Ever since I wrote my thesis and received the grades that I did, I have made being a constructive life-choice maker a premier behavioral script in my repertoire. I can tell you from personal experience that my making the most of a disappointing situation instilled highly positive feelings of accomplishment, self-determinism, and valid pride that I made the most of an unfavorable situation into my *Heart-of-Hearts*. It showed me that I could take constructive and highly positive ownership of any situation that I'm faced with. I just had to figure out the most constructive game plan to achieve the most positive result and then effectively implement it. Having the requisite amount of self-love in my *Heart-of-Hearts* certainly played a major role in my making the right life choice in this situation.

As I mentioned above, because I was inspired to study law as a result of writing my college thesis on the sociological dynamics of juror selection, I enrolled and went to Cornell Law School. The highly disappointing news was that, while I found the day-to-day study of law fairly interesting, it was by no means exciting or stimulating for me. What made matters worse was that I worked for a corporate law firm the summer following my second year at law school and realized that practicing corporate law was absolutely NOT in the cards for me, as it didn't take advantage of my personal skill sets, professional passions, and abilities. Essentially, I realized I would be miserable working for a corporate law firm and would therefore be a mediocre, uninspired attorney. I found myself at a crossroads and needed to ask myself: "Do I continue to attend law school, continue to pay good money (my tuition) after bad, waste valuable time studying for a profession that I will probably never enter, and put off moving toward some other profession or career by staying in law school until after graduation? Or, do I stay in law school and continue to learn as much as I can, focus more on contract law, which does interest me, get my law degree, and make the best of what appears to be a dead-end situation?"

After giving the options great thought, I decided that the constructive choice was to be disciplined and finish what I had started and get my law degree, which could be of value to me and a potential employer later on down the road. I thereby immersed myself in contract law. As it turned out, this choice turned out to be extremely beneficial, as I was introduced to the president of the world-renowned William Morris Agency a few months after graduation, and he loved my interest in contract law and proposed that he craft a career path for me at his firm by being a business affairs contract attorney and eventually a talent representative.

When I heard about all of the illustrious individuals that the William Morris Agency had worked with—the Beatles, Elvis Presley, Robert Redford, Clint Eastwood, Barbara Walters, Al Pacino, Billy Joel, the Beach Boys, and the like—I was sold. I loved the idea that I could work with such talented individuals in enabling them to fulfill their huge and exciting potentials. When I joined the agency, I quickly learned that much of the day-to-day work the agents and their business affairs teammates did was negotiating and securing contracts—contracts between the agency and its clients, and contracts between the clients and the studios, networks, concert promoters, theater owners, commercial producers or sponsors, etc. So being an adept and sage contract attorney was essential. As it turned out, my first big assignment at William Morris was being the business affairs attorney who would oversee all of the staff employment agreements for the new *David Letterman Show* that William Morris represented and would derive huge commissions from. I knew that this was a big opportunity to prove myself to my employers, so I poured myself into the assignment. Fortunately, everything went exceedingly well, and David's widely respected manager, Jack Rollins, sent a note to the president of William Morris detailing what a wonderful job I did as their business affairs liaison. This kind letter and praise were helpful in my being promoted to be one of two individuals that the president would train to one day run the company.

As it turned out, my passion was to represent talented individuals and strategically develop their careers by guiding them in making highly beneficial life and career choices. When I became a news agent, I instantly was accorded great respect and credibility for my contract expertise. My legal training was and has always been an invaluable career asset. All this to say, I'm so grateful and glad that I made the constructive decision to stay in law school and make the best of what seemed to be a no-win situation by heavily focusing on contract law.

PUTTING FAMILY FIRST

I have one more personal story to share with you. Before the pandemic hit, my wife, Melinda, and our two college freshmen, Mary and Tristan, had great plans and hopes to do many exciting things over the next year or so. But as was the case with everyone, our plans had to be scrapped, and intense quarantining took their place. As in the Maccabiah Games situation, I needed to figure out what the most constructive plan of action would be for me. After giving the situation a good deal of thought, I figured out the best new game plan and use of my time:

- Spend as much quality time with my family, as this would probably be the last time that we would enjoy the blessing of spending a great deal of time together in our home.

- Revamp the way my broadcast representation firm operates its business, so that working from a central office would no longer be a necessity.

- Finish writing my book *Career Choreography*.

- If the pandemic lasts longer than expected, write *Aspire Higher*.

As it turned out, the pandemic did last longer than expected, and I am proud to say that I made the most of our many months of quarantining by accomplishing all of my goals.

KEYS TO SECURING POSITIVE OUTCOMES

The moral of these happy-ending stories is that life can certainly throw you curves, and the most well-conceived plans and expectations will need to be altered. The keys to securing a positive and successful outcome when this happens are:

- Commit yourself, even when you are disheartened, to being as constructive and adaptable as possible under any and all circumstances. Deb Mayworm, former president and treasurer of Women of Reform Judaism, so sagely observed that "if you're flexible, you'll never be bent out of shape." So be intellectually and emotionally adaptable.

- Trust that during challenging times, if you do the right, highly constructive things and are disciplined when it's called for, good things will happen. Please see the discussion of my Just-Trust philosophy below.

- Astutely and creatively figure out what being constructive means in the situation you're faced with.

- Effectively implement your constructive choices and steps.

Unquestionably, things don't always go as planned or hoped for. The key is to be as positive, adaptable, and constructive as possible in each situation, and thereby time after time instill more and more empowering, positive feelings into your *Heart-of-Hearts*.

Remember, you can choose to be positive, flexible, and constructive. *Be the Change You Want to See!* A core concept of *The PLCP Lifestyle* is that you take positive, highly constructive ownership of the things that you CAN control, such as your choices, your actions, your mindset, your perspective, and your emotions. As you have read, the spirit of self-determinism pervades *Positive Life Choice Psychology*. That said, in life, no matter how well-thought-out your plans, strategies, and visions for the future are, some things just aren't meant to happen, or at least are not meant to happen on your timetable.

JUST-TRUST PHILOSOPHY

Sometimes, you are destined to experience the unforeseen or unexpected. This turn of events, however, can very well turn out in the big picture of your life to be far more beneficial and instructive for you than what you had originally envisioned or planned. Therefore, when your life zigs when you were expecting and hoping for it to zag, trust that there are reasons for this, and do your best to make the most of the detour.

I have personally experienced and observed throughout my life that certain seemingly undesirable events took place in my life and in the lives of others that in hindsight were essential life lessons for us to learn and experience, so that we could continue to positively grow, evolve, and thrive.

I am a huge proponent of the insights "Everything in its own time" and "Patience is a virtue." I have found and counseled that no matter how well and astutely planned your life game plan is, there are times when you must be patient and let go of your plans and expectations, and willingly and confidently accept the sometimes uncertain flow of life. This is my Just-Trust philosophy, in that when things go awry, just trust and be at peace with the concept that if you do the right and constructive things in these instances, then positive or at least necessary experiences and lessons for your growth will be the result.

There will be events that you can't control. We must graciously accept and embrace this reality for our mental, emotional, and physical well-being. This sentiment is oh so eloquently reflected in the prayer: "God, grant me the serenity to accept the things I cannot change, the courage to change the things I can, and the wisdom to know the difference." The secular version of this prayer is one in which you adopt these peace-providing qualities. Embracing this perspective will make your life better and healthier in so many ways.

The key is to strike a positive balance between making the most of what you can control, and constructively accepting and adapting to what God, fate, or whatever force you believe in has in store for you. As you undoubtedly have heard many times before, "Man/woman makes plans, and God laughs!" So be ready for the inevitable zigs and zags of life, accept them, and make the most of them.

Another peace-providing philosophy is not to worry about everything that might go wrong in the future. During my life and my long positive-life-choice counseling career, I have observed that so many individuals were brought down psychologically, emotionally, and spiritually because they worried and fretted about future issues over which they had no control. In many instances, these individuals suffered tremendous anxiety and fear regarding potential events that never came to fruition or turned out differently and far better than they expected, and they wound up spending so much of their precious time worrying and enduring huge consternation for nothing.

Once again, control the things that you can, and regarding the events you can't control, Just-Trust that if you do the right things and constructively accept and adapt to the events in your future, you're making the most of your precious time here on earth.

BE A SOLUTIONARY

Let's now discuss the core *PLCP* concept of being a *solutionary*.

One of the most important concepts I learned in law school is that when you're faced with a problem or challenge, your first step is to "spot the issue." Put another way, once you can accurately assess or identify what your challenge or problem is, you have a far better chance of finding a constructive and beneficial solution. This process is similar to a patient coming to a doctor with a malady. Once the physician can accurately diagnose the illness or problem, she or he should have a far better chance of figuring out an effective cure or remedy. In both of these instances, the attorney and the doctor attempt to find solutions to a problem by first ascertaining what the precise issue is.

Throughout our lives, we are faced with obstacles, challenges, and concerns, and as we discussed in the previous chapter, our goal is to solve the problem or challenge in as constructive a manner as possible. Finding beneficial solutions to problems fills your *Heart-of-Hearts* with empowering feelings of mastery, accomplishment, confidence, and feelings of high self-esteem that will lead you to do more good things for yourself. But just because you have found a solution to a problem or challenge doesn't mean that you're a solutionary. Being a solutionary requires you to aspire higher, as it involves a higher calling.

According to *Psychology Today*, being a "'solutionary' is not synonymous with [being a] 'problem-solver' . . . Solutionaries are motivated by compassion and justice"; they solve problems "in a strategic, comprehensive manner that strives not to harm one group while helping another."[1] The Urban Dictionary defines a solutionary as "someone who finds revolutionary answers to life problems . . . A type of revolutionary who makes change by providing a better way to do things."[2]

For our purposes, being a solutionary means taking into account others' feelings, priorities, and well-being when making our decisions. It requires us to meaningfully and effectively consider others' interests when identifying the best solutions to any problems that we face. Being a solutionary requires that we not only find constructive solutions and beneficial plans of action that enhance and benefit ourselves, but that we also strive to creatively and compassionately devise a means by which our decisions and choices will positively impact and elevate the quality of others' lives.

I have seen in the news business and observed in life that everyone has a compelling and complex life story. In my quest to aspire higher, I strive to objectively hear, absorb, understand, and respect that story so that I'm able to make positive and highly beneficial life choices involving that individual. I believe that going through this beautiful and loving process is a prerequisite for being the most effective solutionary possible.

Being a solutionary will make you feel even better than being an astute constructive decision-maker, because you're taking others' feelings, concerns, and ideas into account when crafting your solutions and actions. These compassionate, empathetic, caring acts will fill your *Heart-of-Hearts* with strong feelings of aspiring higher, of answering a higher calling, of being a truly good, caring, loving person—all HUGELY empowering and self-esteem-raising feelings that will exponentially increase your feelings of self-love and love for others.

Please remember: Your song sounds better when we sing it *together*. Be cognizant of others and their needs and values when making your life choices; be their light! I would like to close this chapter with a poem that I have written for you.

BE THEIR LIGHT

There are times when others are enveloped by fright,
And the present and future seem dark as night,
But know that things will be all right,
As long as you're there to BE THEIR LIGHT.

When others struggle to do what's right,
When they feel lost and all uptight,
And they believe they can't escape their plight,
It's up to you to BE THEIR LIGHT.

And although your motives they may not understand,
As you open your heart and extend your hand,
If fear has blinded them, be their sight,
Guide them through their darkness, BE THEIR LIGHT.

AGAPE LOVE

Love is the ultimate and the highest
goal to which you can aspire
—VIKTOR FRANKL

Act consistently with your
highest self, and the greatest
rewards will be yours!
—KL

Now that we have discussed what being a solutionary entails and that it requires considering the needs, concerns, and well-being of others in conjunction with yours when making your life choices, let's briefly discuss agape love and how it compares with *The Positive Life Choice Psychology*'s Altruistic Love.

"Agape love is selfless, sacrificial, unconditional love. It is the highest of all of the types of love in the Bible." Freelance writer Jessica Tholmer writes that agape love "is universal love," and that "it can be found in the people who dedicate their lives to helping others . . . like teachers, nurses, or people who dedicate themselves to others."[1]

The qualities and aspirations that Ms. Tholmer identifies and discusses are the same as those for *PLCP*'s Altruistic Love. Where agape love and the *PLCP* Altruistic Love seem to differ a bit is that, according to Tholmer, "when you express yourself in terms of agape love, you're putting others before yourself."[2] In the Positive Life Choice Lifestyle, you may well, some of the time, much of the time, or all of the time "put others before yourself," but this is not a requirement of or mandate for Altruistic Love. What you aspire to do in Altruistic Love is to respectfully, lovingly, and compassionately care about, support, consider, and have compassion for others when you make life choices that involve or impact them.

That said, agape love and *PLCP* love both ask you to aspire highest in that you are asked to do things for their intrinsic goodness and to take loving responsibility for the well-being of others, with all acts done unconditionally and with no expected payback, karmic or otherwise. Both loves are ideals to strive for; adopting both loves will fill your *Heart-of-Hearts* with highly empowering positive feelings; and both will lead you to elevate the quality of your life, your psyche and spirit, your self-esteem and self-image, your country and the world. All awesome rewards for being your best self! As we discussed earlier, *The PLCP Lifestyle* supports any set of beliefs, religion, or love that motivates you to aspire higher and be your highest self; so, whether you embrace the *PLCP* Altruistic form of love or that of agape, you are well on your way to filling your *Heart-of-Hearts with the most empowering love* and self-actualizing in the most effective and wonderful ways.

One additional and significant difference between *The PLCP Lifestyle* Altruistic Love and agape love appears to be that with *PLCP* Altruistic Love, you are given clear steps and insights to equip, enable, and empower you to get to the point where you are intellectually, emotionally, and psychologically READY to authentically embrace and organically practice Altruistic Love on a sustained basis. For many individuals, figuratively flipping an epiphanic intellectual switch and saying that "I'm ready to start practicing unconditional love today" is unrealistic, as their *Heart-of-Hearts* isn't yet truly open and fortified enough with the all-important feelings of self-love and self-worth so that they can with great effectiveness and consistency succeed in their noble quest to love unconditionally. We must first build a rock-solid foundation of strong, personal inner love by taking the right disciplined steps before we can attain and consistently practice authentic, unconditional love. This is why and where *Aspire Higher* and *The Positive Life Choice Psychology* are so essential for your true, sustained growth no matter what form of unconditional love you ultimately adopt and embrace.

HINENI

*H*ineni is a Hebrew word that means "I am here!" or "I am present!" It's such a simple word that conjures up so many positive and constructive messages and outlines an ideal, pure way to live your life. For *The PLCP Lifestyle*, the word hineni can mean:

- I am present and living in the moment. I'm not dwelling on the past and what could have been or what didn't go right. No "wouldas, shouldas, or couldas for me. I'm not going to be brought down by the past. I'm putting the past in my rearview mirror and driving forward with great commitment, optimism, and hope. I'm blessed to be alive today and going to make the very most of this day and every day."

  I'm also not fixated on worrying about the future. "Yesterday is history; tomorrow is a mystery; and all I have is today, which is why they call it 'the present.'"[1]

  When it comes to individuals passing, the Greeks didn't care how a person died, but whether they truly lived. Living in the moment and for all moments puts you in the best position to be able to say, with great pride and satisfaction, that "I left it all out on the court during my lifetime."

- I am mindful. Being mindful, once again, connotes living in the moment and being aware. This includes being aware of when you are enveloped in emotions that could cause you to make a poor or destructive choice or act in an inappropriate, harmful, or self-sabotaging manner, such as lashing out at someone, retaliating, or pushing the send button, whereas in a cooler and clearer moment, you would wisely refrain from doing all of these things. Being mindful can mean taking others' feelings, concerns, needs, and ideas into account when making your choices and figuring out ways to solve problems. As we discussed, having concern and compassion for others, and doing one's best to picture what walking in another person's shoes entails, is what separates problem-solvers from solutionaries.

- I am cognitively clear. I am committed to recognizing when the negativity bias is coloring my perspective and am attuned to making sure that I don't go into Negative Town with my attitude, outlook, and decision-making. This proactive vigilance, along with getting enough sleep and filling my *Heart-of-Hearts* with positives so that the negative can't get in or take hold, are highly effective means to ward off and negate the negativity bias. However, should you feel yourself succumbing to the negativity bias, proactively center yourself by meditating, lifting your spirits by acknowledging and savoring your blessings, watching a positive show or film, playing music that puts you in a positive mood, and the like.[1] The key is to take your mind off the negative and reframe what you might perceive as a negative situation into a more positive and constructive one.[2] Being present, mindful, and in the moment can be hugely beneficial when staving off the deleterious effects of the negativity bias.

I am here! Yes, you are! And you can make such a positive difference by who you are, in the values you adopt and practice, the examples you set, the people and spirits you lift through your acts and words of kindness, your compassion and love, and the way you live your life and conduct your business. You can be a radiant light and wellspring of support and encouragement for others, as well as the nurturing wind beneath their wings.

Always remember the word hineni and think: I am here! I'm dialed in. I'm engaged. I'm going to aspire higher and make a positive difference and impact. HINENI! I AM HERE AND I'M GOING TO MAKE IT COUNT!

THE CONTINUAL GATHERING, ANALYSIS, AND INTEGRATION OF NEW DATA

There is no more important tool for positive growth, change, and constructive decision-making than the strategy of continuing throughout your life to gather and analyze new data—ideas, experiences, insights, and knowledge—and then testing that data against what you already know, believe, and employ in your day-to-day life. Some of the questions that you can ask include: How does the new data compare to the data on which you based your prior decision? Is it better, more advantageous, and/or healthier for you? Will it be more helpful in attaining your goals? Does it enhance you? If the answers are affirmative, you must then decide how to most effectively integrate these insights, first into your thought and decision-making processes, and then into your behavioral repertoire.

As people who know me well will attest, the foundation for almost all of my real-life navigation skills and decision-making strategies has come from my athletic experiences, specifically those in tennis and POP Tennis. Unlike sports such as baseball, basketball, and football, where you have coaches on the sidelines to guide and counsel you, and others can come in for you if you're having a bad day, as a singles player in tennis, you are out there alone. You have only yourself to rely on. If you're tired, sick, or having a rough day, either you suck it up, adapt, and get it right, or you lose. There's no one on the bench to come in and take your place. It's the true survival of the fitter, smarter, more technically proficient, more emotionally intelligent, and more creative competitor. As a result of participating in these individual sports, I've learned to become self-reliant and self-deterministic—because if you don't figure it out and do it right, no one else will do it for you.

When I'm on the tennis court playing singles, I have to continually assimilate data as I make my strategic decisions. For example, where is the sun and how will it affect me and my opponent when we serve? What kind of surface are we playing on (e.g., clay, cement, grass, synthetic), how fast or slow will the ball play on the court, and how will this information affect me and my opponent? Which direction is the wind blowing? What are my opponent's strengths and weaknesses, the knowledge of which I have gleaned from past experience, my research, and/or watching him/her during our prematch warmup? Depending upon how the match progresses, which of my strategies should I continue to rely on, abandon, and/or modify?

In the Jewish religion, there are two "High Holidays," Rosh Hashanah and Yom Kippur. Rosh Hashanah is the Jewish New Year and begins a ten-day period of self-reflection and study. It is intended to be an honest, guilt-free examination of what the observing individual has done right and well during the past year, and done incorrectly or could have been done better or perhaps omitted altogether. At the heart of this study is the premise that we are all human beings, and we will never be perfect. We have and will continue to make mistakes; they are to be expected. The key to healthy emotional and psychological growth is not to be brought down by or dwell on your missteps, but rather to learn from them and thereby grow to be a better, wiser, and more thoughtful and compassionate individual each year.

The ten-day period of reflection and study ends on Yom Kippur. At sunset on Yom Kippur, a horn called a shofar is blown, signifying that a new year has begun, and the gift of a brand-new figurative canvas has been given to each of us to paint on. The hope is that we will all evolve to be wiser and more loving, caring, compassionate, empathetic, and humane artists with each passing year.

The PLCP Philosophy suggests that every day presents us with a Rosh Hashanah and a Yom Kippur: we must constantly be open to objectively and nondefensively gathering new data and new perspectives, and gleaning greater understanding of and keener insights regarding ourselves, others, and life. We must continually reexamine and objectively compare our old and current behavioral strategies, as well as our beliefs and perspectives of ourselves and others, to see if they are still appropriate and the best and most enhancing ones for us. We must consciously and continuously strive to be better, smarter, more evolved, and more understanding of everything and everyone around us. How you analyze and integrate the information you've gathered into your thought processes and behavioral repertoire will be uniquely yours, and it should also reflect your highest personal ideals, self, and values. Optimally, you will create and re-create strategies moving forward that will be effective and constructive for you and others, and will elevate and enhance you and others.

As always, if you can make choices that enhance you as well as others, you will fill your *Heart-of-Hearts* with the kind of positive energy that will lead you to make more and more strong and loving choices that will benefit and lift you, others, and the world we live in. So be the most radiant light possible in your life and in as many other lives as possible.

In discussing the High Holidays of Rosh Hashanah and Yom Kippur, I mentioned that when we review both what we've done right and could have done differently or better, the process is guilt- and fear-free. ("No sins—just wins!") It is all about learning, growing, and improving. When you make a faux pas, understand it, analyze it, and learn from it. Then put it in your rearview mirror and drive with great optimism toward wiser and more evolved days.

In a recent conversation that I had with Rabbi David Woznica, he explained that the process of Leonardo da Vinci painting the Mona Lisa is much like the ten-day period of self-examination that we just discussed. With infrared light, one can see the many times that da Vinci painted an imperfect stroke, which he later painted over in an effort to improve it. In some cases, da Vinci had to paint over a stroke many times until he felt that he had finally gotten it right. Rabbi Woznica analogizes this process to our making and taking imperfect choices and steps, respectively, and continually improving them until we finally get them right. The key is to lovingly and constructively aspire higher by taking the steps that will enable us to be our best selves and attain our greatest potentials.

A second point that Rabbi Woznica made is that with the naked eye we only see the finished, masterful final product that da Vinci ultimately produced, and not the many times that he had to start over, regroup, and improve. So we must not be discouraged or intimidated when we see the final, stellar version of a person, product, or process; it's essential to understand that success is attained through a journey of starting over, rethinking, regrouping, taking necessary steps back in order to take enhancing and beneficial steps forward, and improving. It's all part of the constructive life process of growing and evolving.

TAKING PRIORITIZATION TIME

A longtime friend who has grown to be one of this country's most innovative, astute, and successful business creators shared with me that each day, for twenty minutes or so, he clears his agenda and his mind, and takes quiet time to come up with new business ideas. He thinks about needs, voids, and potential new niches in the marketplace and then figures out ways to effectively fill them. Similarly, if you can take time each day to relax and declutter from the "whole lotta-nada" that is swirling in your head, and think about the people who are important to you, what truly matters, and how you can be the most caring and evolved individual possible, so many wonderful, positive future choices and actions can be the beautiful result. This quiet prioritization time will be invaluable to you and to the others whose lives you touch as you aspire higher.

MOTIVATION AND ENERGY-CHARGE EXPRESSION

Let's now focus on and keep in mind **three levels of motivation and energy-charge expression:**

1. The lowest level of motivation and energy-charge expression is **performing acts out of fear, guilt, sadness, loneliness, hurt, anger, and hate**. For example, when one acts out of fear, whether the fear of punishment or getting caught, the motive for acting in such a manner isn't highly evolved.

2. The next level of motivation is when you perform acts with "karma" as your incentive. That is, you perform a certain act because you expect or hope for something good to come back to you in return. And while I believe that "karma" in some form does exist and acting in hopes of a

"karmic payback" is more evolved than acting out of, say, fear or guilt, such acting or giving can in most instances be "conditional."

3. As we have discussed, the highest level of motivation and energy-charge expression in *The PLCP Lifestyle* is **acting altruistically**. This is the goal. Altruistic acts are performed purely because they are intrinsically the right things to do, with no regard for any benefit that you might receive for performing them. These acts are undertaken lovingly, selflessly, and unconditionally.

As it turns out, you do receive an incredible benefit when you engage in the altruistic acts of Toxic Energy Charge Dissipation, such as loving, forgiving, understanding, respecting others, and being compassionate, sympathetic, and empathetic. When you perform these acts, they not only dissipate your highly toxic energy charges, but they fill your *Heart-of-Hearts* with positive feelings about and perceptions of yourself, which in turn catalyze you to make more positive choices and take more positive actions. So, one positive choice and act organically leads you to make other positive ones, while you continue to fill your *Heart-of-Hearts* with feelings of high self-worth.

The more you have feelings of high self-worth, the more you develop and feel the empowering feelings of self-love, and once you feel true self-love, you are far more likely to be forgiving and understanding of others and yourself, as well as loving, respectful, and compassionate. So, one process (utilizing *TECD*) is completely complementary to the other (instilling positive feelings and perceptions into your *Heart-of-Hearts*).

Additionally, by unconditionally forgiving, understanding, respecting, appreciating, and loving others, and showing compassion and empathy/sympathy for them, you put the percentages strongly in your favor that you will more easily and effectively diffuse your toxic energy charges.

It has been said that "forgiveness is a favor that you do for yourself"[1] and that "showing grace is giving someone the benefit of the doubt."[2] Unquestionably, expressing forgiveness, concern, compassion, empathy, and the like empowers you with the high turbo-charged positive feelings within to aspire higher, be your best self, and enjoy your best life . . . all while helping, supporting, and elevating others. How supremely great is that?

TRUE HAPPINESS
AND BEING FULFILLED

*Life is never made unbearable by
circumstances, but only by lack of
meaning and purpose.*
—VIKTOR FRANKL

Many of us spend a tremendous portion of our lives working, and if your *Heart-of-Hearts* is going to be filled with feelings of love, high self-esteem, confidence, and other positives, it's important to like or love what you do professionally.

In my book *Career Choreography: Your Step-by-Step Guide to Finding the Right Job and Achieving Huge Success and Happiness*, I discuss how essential it is to find a position or profession that you love or like, one that you're good at or have the strong potential to be good at, and one that takes advantage of your skill sets, education, and/ or experience. And, if you are truly fortunate and an astute career choreographer, the job or position will also "make your heart sing"![1]

Don Browne, whom I mentioned earlier, generously shared with me his sage **criteria for someone identifying the right job, position, or career** for them. Here they are:[2]

- Do what you believe in.

- Do what you love.

- Do what gives you something to look forward to every day.

I absolutely agree with Don's list, and I would add a fourth criterion:

- Do something that is of service to and benefits and lifts others.

These criteria make me think of my best friend Joe, who was my wonderful college roommate. While in his thirties, Joe quit his position as a comptroller of a major national company to become a high school teacher and help his accomplished wife, Lanie, raise their three terrific daughters. Joe, who is now retired, taught because he truly loved it, and from all accounts, he inspired and unconditionally supported a plethora of students on both the east and west coasts. By teaching and thereby having more time to spend with his family after school, on weekends, and during the summer, he was also able to be the loving and fully engaged husband and father that makes his heart sing, as well as the full hearts of his family.

By consciously choosing to leave his prestigious position as a comptroller, Joe earned less money, but he enhanced so many people around him, all of whom are happier and better off for having known him. Put another way, Joe and Lanie chose to give up some financial security so that Joe could spend more time with their children to solidify their emotional security. As a committed educator and loving husband and father, Joe was true to himself as he recognized and pursued his calling. For as long as he's been a teacher, Joe has always been fulfilled and enjoyed radiant inner peace. He is one of my heroes.

As I reviewed the above four criteria, I realized that they are also the recipe for a happy, meaningful, and emotionally and psychologically healthy life. If in your life you do what you believe in, what you love, what you look forward to doing, and what helps and elevates others, you are truly acting consistently with your highest and most self-empowering values and manifesting your highest self. All of these acts and feelings will enable you to effectively and plentifully fill your *Heart-of-Hearts* with beautiful positives.

Please remember, your valid feelings of being proud of how you conduct your life are invaluable in lifting the quality of your life, the lives of others with whom you interact, and our society.

THE GREAT IMPORTANCE OF "EPIGENETICS"

An abundance of compelling scientific evidence exists as to why you want to experience sustained inner happiness, serenity, and fulfillment, which comes from the burgeoning field of epigenetics. Years ago, the prevailing belief was that "your DNA is your unalterable destiny," meaning that the positive and negative traits that you inherit and are encoded in your DNA are etched in stone and unchangeable. However, according to relatively recent epigenetic research, some "environmental" factors can modify your genes' activity; or put another way, each of us inherits a certain genetic code or sequence at conception. But whether a particular gene is activated or not, and how it is expressed, can be directly influenced by the choices that we make, what we eat or don't eat, what toxins we are exposed to, and the thoughts, feelings, and stresses that we harbor. These environmental influences can either turn off or activate certain genes in your body so that you will be far more likely to contract cancer or diabetes, suffer from depression, a stroke, or bipolar disorder, and be vulnerable to myriad other diseases and disorders.[3]

Equally important is that the epigenetic changes that result from how you *think and feel,* as well as from how you eat and what you are exposed to, can be passed down to your children and generations thereafter.[4]

What is so remarkable about the science of epigenetics is that it teaches us that we can change the way that a gene is expressed or behaves without changing an inherited genetic sequence. Epigenetics gives you the means and the power to change the destiny of your and your offspring's health, emotional and psychological wellness, and your longevity by how you think, view events and others, and make choices. Therefore, you want to live a life filled with love, peace, tranquility, and goodness, free from abundant stress, anger, bitterness, and hate. Similarly, being of service to others, whether professionally or personally, and feeling fulfilled by it may well enhance and be highly beneficial for your epigenetic process. So, once again, instilling love into your *Heart-of-Hearts*, psyche, and life and making positive life choices is highly beneficial and healthy both for you and your children.

A few final thoughts. If you desire to truly enjoy and derive great fulfillment from your professional life, then do something you love, believe in, and that makes you look forward to going to work every day, but also take a job that maximizes your abilities, work, and educational experiences. Visualize a professional football or basketball coach whose job it is to put his or her players in positions that make the most of those players' particular skills, talents, and assets. That coach may also construct a "system" or game plan that brings out the best in his or her players. To make the most of your professional gifts and to self-actualize, you must be your own insightful and effective professional coach by making sure that you are in a job, position, or profession that makes the most of and showcases your particular strengths. Just as a particular system in sports can increase the players' chances of attaining highly rewarding success, the job you're in should be one that you will likely excel in and derive great job satisfaction from. If you do this, you are well on your way to enjoying a highly fulfilling and rewarding professional life. You spend so much of your time working, you will be best served by doing something that makes your heart sing.

All that said, during the pandemic, so many individuals have lost their jobs, their incomes, their productivity, their confidence to efficaciously recover from severe blows, and their hope. No doubt, these are exceedingly hard and difficult times. But as someone who has been successfully choreographing and developing careers for over thirty-five years, I also view this as your golden opportunity to take stock of what would make you truly happy professionally and to engage in a wonderful professional reset. Personally, some difficult and unsettling things happened to me when I was working for a major entertainment firm about thirty-four years ago that made me consider something I never would have if things had been going smoothly—that is, leave the big firm and start my own company. After giving this option great thought, I did start my own company, and it has turned out to be one of the best decisions I have ever made. I'm exponentially happier and truly love what I do each day.

I believe that things happen for a reason, and the reason I was experiencing such an unhappy and frustrating time at my old job was that I needed a strong incentive and push to make a life-changing, career-enhancing move, which I probably wouldn't have made otherwise. Similarly, maybe the reason you were laid off or let go is because you are meant to reexamine your professional path and aspire higher by identifying and securing a position that is much more rewarding, soul-nourishing, and spirit-lifting. When I counsel my clients, as they try to put into the proper perspective why they had to endure the devastating event of losing their jobs, I suggest that sometimes you have to take a step or two back in order to take five fulfilling steps forward. The key here is to figure out what you most want in a new position and what your skill sets and work and educational experiences have prepared you to do. Then strategically find and secure the job that will elevate your spirits, your soul, and your happiness.

A related thought is that during the pandemic and post-pandemic periods, we all have experienced, personally or through observation, the fragility of life and health. As a result, people now crave more professional fulfillment, a better work-life balance, or to be closer to and/or spend more time with family. I have had so many clients and friends express these strong, gnawing sentiments to me. If you are feeling this way, this is your golden time and opportunity to aspire higher and make a spirit-enriching professional pivot.

Just the other day, "Jacqueline" sought my counsel, as she wanted much more soul satisfaction from her job. Jacqueline is a well-paid, highly successful litigation attorney living in the Midwest. When I asked her what she would love to do, she, with great zest and conviction, said that she would love to become a junior high school teacher and make a positive difference in young people's lives; she would love to be closer to her aging parents, who live in Utah; and her dream has always been to be a swimming coach for those who desire to compete, as she grew up as a competitive swimmer and it is in her blood.

After listening to Jacqueline and seeing and feeling the pure excitement in her voice and in her demeanor as she described her ideal life, I could easily suggest that she give up, as she had described it to me, "the rat race of the business world" and move to Utah so that she could live her dreams of being a teacher, being close to and enjoying her aging parents and siblings, and on weekends and after school, be a competitive swimming coach. I punctuated my idea by saying, "Jacqueline, your parents won't be around forever. If not now, when [will you make this highly beneficial move]?"

A few days later, Jacqueline called to tell me that she was over the moon, as she was going to make the move to Utah in the next couple of months. I'm elated for her!

If you are feeling like so many others do, that there's a position out there that's more meaningful, more fulfilling, more in harmony with who you truly are or want to be, then it may well be time to make a life-enhancing professional move . . . because, if not now, when?

SHALOM

One of the most beautiful and impactful words I know is "shalom," which is Hebrew for "hello," "goodbye," "peace," "harmony," "wholeness," "completeness," "prosperity," and "tranquility."[1] There is something so beautiful about saying hello and goodbye to someone with a word that means peace, harmony, and tranquility. If everyone would wish all others peace, harmony, and tranquility when they meet, speak, part, or correspond . . . how wonderful and peace-evoking would that be?

I would certainly suggest that the more you say the word "peace," offer peace, think about the beauty of peace . . . the more it becomes a prominent and treasured value in your consciousness and way of life.

At a time when our country and our world are being torn apart by anger, vitriol, and violence, the beautiful, unifying qualities of inner peace, serenity, completeness, and wholeness, as well as world peace, harmony, and tranquility, are states of being that we all with great passion and commitment must strive to attain and maintain.

Shalom!

THE AWESOME WEIGHT
OF EXPECTATIONS

I would like to share a couple of relevant stories with you regarding how others' expectations can negatively affect you, your growth, and your well-being.

My grandfather died when my father was four years old. Thereafter, he and his family moved to the United States. By the time my dad was fourteen, he was working full time, helping to support his family. In a true "Horatio Alger" scenario, he progressed from a stock boy to executive vice president of a prominent department-store chain. Because my dad had to work full time at such an early age, he never even attended high school. As a result, he always felt insecure about the fact that he didn't have the formal education that those above, around, and below him at his company had. There were times when my dad had offers to join other firms and had backers who wanted him to strike out on his own. However, he chose to stay with his company, as security was of the greatest importance and a preeminent value to him. As a result, he wasn't inclined to take any significant professional risks.

In my sophomore year of college, I had a chance to be coached by Gardnar Mulloy (a former world-class tennis champion) and to play on the international tennis circuit. The hitch was that I would have to quit college ASAP and play tennis full time. When I told my dad about my opportunity, he froze with fear and anger. He couldn't talk. His son was now at Harvard and would almost certainly have great prospects and a secure life upon graduation. This was more than my father could ever have hoped for. The thought of me leaving Harvard left my dad speechless. After an endless moment, he responded angrily, "You've got it all going for you. Are you going to throw it all away to be a tennis bum? Do you want to teach tennis the rest of your life, under the hot sun, and dry up like a prune?"

He walked away in apparent disgust. I believe that my dad was scared to death that I would make a horrible life decision. For about a week, he couldn't talk to me. Gardnar suggested that I could always go back to school later, but when it comes to athletics, I had to give it my best shot while I was still young. He was right. Gardnar concluded by saying, "Before you reach your decision, you should remember one thing: 'It's the things that you never do, that you'll always regret.'" I believe that he was not entirely right on this one, as I've been invited to go bungee jumping a couple of times, and declined the offer each time, with no regrets. However, all in all, this was pretty heavy and heady stuff for a nineteen-year-old to be deciding. As my mom was sensitive to my love of athletics and the need to go for it while you're young, she said that she would support me in whatever I chose—as long as I thought things out carefully and clearly.

I did. I acknowledged that I was starting to enjoy my pre-law studies as much as, or more than, playing tennis. (POP Tennis was another matter. Too bad I couldn't play POP Tennis professionally. That would have made for a really tough decision!) I took time to reflect upon what my true passions were at that moment, and I realized that my priorities and what I valued the most seemed to be changing. I was incredibly excited about writing my senior thesis on decision-making and the sociological selection of jurors. I also had experienced ligament problems in one of my ankles during the past couple of years. As a result, I wasn't sure that my body would be able to withstand the grueling punishment of practicing and competing each day. And, when I got right down to it, in my *Heart-of-Hearts*, I *knew* that no matter how good I was as a tennis player, I didn't think I'd become good enough to enjoy consistent success on the pro tour.

On the other hand, athletics had been my life. They were inextricably intertwined with my identity and my sense of self. Athletics, for the most part, helped me change from being a heavy, clumsy, insecure child to a thinner, more agile, accomplished young adult. Being an athlete made me stand out and made me special. I liked Gardnar's idea of going back to school if things didn't work out, or even if they did. What a freeing and exciting way to live, playing tennis all over the world, being coached for a year or so by world-renowned Gardnar Mulloy.

It sounded great . . . but it didn't sound right.

On the last day of my two-week trip to Florida, Gardnar and I played an exhibition match at the Fontainebleau Hotel in Miami Beach, where he was director of tennis, and my parents and I were staying. During the two weeks of playing tennis full time and being coached by Gardnar, my game rose almost two levels. I felt like I was playing the best tennis of my life. I continued to play well, as I started the exhibition match by jumping off to a quick lead.

Then suddenly, it all caved in. I had to face what my final decision had to be. I was going back to school. Later that day, I would leave sunny skies and the eighty-degree weather of Miami Beach to return to snowy, cold Massachusetts to (catch up on my work and) study for final exams. There would be no more intense practice sessions coached by Gardnar. Studying would once again take clear priority. Within days of returning to school, my game would begin to slip. It had to. For the next four weeks or so, I could, at best, play an hour or two of tennis a couple of times each week. That's no way to raise your game. Gardnar's words came crashing through my mind: "It's the things that you never do, that you'll always regret." I began to lose track of the exhibition match. If I wasn't crying on the outside, I certainly was crying within. I didn't win another game the rest of the match. I couldn't stand to see myself playing so well . . . as it would all be for naught.

That evening, Gardnar drove me to the airport. He could tell that I had made up my mind. As we parted, he gave me a copy of the book that he had written, *The Will to Win*. In it he inscribed his prophetic words, "It's the things that you never do . . ."

As I boarded the plane to Boston, I knew that I had just closed the door on the most sacred and cherished part of my life to date: the beauty, passion, and pure innocence of seriously pursuing athletics.

On the plane, as I thumbed through Gardnar's book, I reflected on the fact that I had reached my decision *not* because of the pressure put on me by my dad, but because of my own heartfelt reasons. Earlier that day, I had told my parents of my decision. My dad was thrilled, and I truly understood why. My mom wanted to be sure that I was comfortable with my decision. She asked if I was sad. I said that I was but that I had made the right choice.

However, it was not until two years later that I learned a huge lesson. It was the night that I played the first of my two exhibition matches against Arthur Ashe, and won! After that match, my dad was as shocked and as proud as he could be. He walked up to me, kissed and hugged me, and commented, "Maybe you should have played professional tennis."

Oh my God! So many things ran through my mind at that moment. Things like "So *now* I get it. You didn't want me to pursue tennis, because *you* didn't think that *I* was good enough." And, "Great! Two years later, when I no longer have Gardnar to coach me, and I've lost two un-recoupable years of development, you start to have an open mind!"

Upon reflection, I came to the following conclusions:

- Though my dad really loved me, he saw things out of his (subjective) eyes—eyes that valued security over almost anything else. As he often feared that he might not be "good enough," he feared that I, too, might not be good enough. He feared that I would throw everything away—everything that I (and he) had worked for. But his values didn't coincide with and reflect my values. At that moment I decided that from now on, when listening to his advice, I must always take this into account.

- Had I decided not to pursue playing tennis full time strictly because I would have incurred my dad's disapproval, I would have been devastated after beating Arthur Ashe and hearing my dad say, "Maybe you should have gone for it." The lesson that I learned that evening was to make decisions and strive for goals based on values that I can live with, because I am the one who has to live with them for the rest of my life. I realized that my dad's and mom's perspectives aren't always right for me. And as I get older and grow to be wiser about myself, there will be times when I'm going to have to make decisions that they won't agree with. And I will—because sometimes, "Child knows best!" (What's in his or her own *Heart-of-Hearts*.)

- I also realized that I had reached the right decision two years earlier (not to pursue tennis in lieu of attending college), when my victory over Arthur and my dad's startling remark didn't make me second-guess myself. My decision had been based upon good reasoning and an accurate perception of where my true interests and priorities were heading, as well as my correct assessment that I wouldn't be consistently successful on any level of the pro tennis tour.

While growing up, we are subject to expectations put on us by our parents or primary caregivers, spouses, partners, and significant others, friends, teachers, advisors, loved ones, employers, etc. (As an only child, I might well have been subject to even more and greater expectations.) Through these and other experiences, I learned that when reaching my decisions, I must not let those expectations lead me to make flawed or destructive decisions. It's gratifying and fun to live up to or exceed someone's or society's expectations, but only if my decisions and actions are healthy and constructive for me in my life. Please remember the praise, accolades, and applause for a crowd-pleasing choice last only for a fleeting moment, and then when the dust settles, you're stuck with your good or bad decision—possibly for your lifetime. This is an essential life lesson.

I cannot count the number of individuals who made crucial, life-changing decisions, such as pursuing a particular career path, because they were trying to please their parents, spouses, or partners, who ended up deeply regretting their decisions and lot in life. Because these individuals were implicitly or explicitly forced to live someone else's dream, toxic feelings of bitterness, anger, resentment, and rage are now embedded in these individuals' *Heart-of-Hearts*. This has been a profoundly sad reality for me and others who care about them to see.

After my Arthur Ashe victory, on a cerebral level, I understood that I can't always attain my father's approval when I make my life choices, and I was okay with that. I could handle it! Or so I thought, until I realized how much my dad's approval truly meant to me. I'll never forget the Tuesday morning during my senior year of college, when I was home visiting my parents during a semester study break. My dad and I were having breakfast at the local diner. We were talking about how well college was going and that I would be busy that weekend, writing essays for my law school applications. My father casually said, "Could you imagine if you got into Harvard Law School?" I could see the great excitement in his eyes as he pictured that event.

I quickly changed the subject, and we went on with our conversation. I spent the rest of the day writing and never gave the morning's talk another thought.

But that night, at about three a.m., I woke up violently shaking in my bed, with my shirt, shorts, and sheets drenched in sweat. I couldn't stop shaking. It was as if I were playing Linda Blair's role in *The Exorcist*, and I was possessed by an unrelenting, deeply ingrained demon. And in some sense, I was.

I waited to see if I could calm down. I couldn't. My whole body was a tremor. I felt like crying. In my *Heart-of-Hearts*, I felt incredible sadness and some anger.

Amazingly, I knew exactly what the cause was. I walked into my parents' bedroom, woke them up, and said, "Dad, I need to talk to you. I'm *not* going to get into Harvard Law School. I'm just not!" I continued to shake as tears welled up in my eyes.

After a moment or two, I gained a bit more composure and said, "Dad, I got into Harvard because I was well-rounded. But there are so many guys applying from Harvard undergrad to Harvard Law School who are far better law board test (LSAT) takers than I am. Harvard Law School will accept only a few guys from Harvard undergrad, and I know that I'll need between a 760 and an 800 on my LSATs to qualify. I've never tested *that* well. I *won't* get in, and you need to know it. I'm sorry."

My mom, shocked, exclaimed, "Kenny, you're shaking and soaking wet!" My father, visibly angry with himself for having caused me such pain, exhorted, with as much passion as I've ever seen, "Kenny, listen to me! First of all, what kind of a son-of-a-gun am I to put pressure on you? I've had almost no education. I was happy for you to go to Harvard because I wanted you to have the education I never had. The education that would allow you to do things I never could. I've gotten by with smoke and mirrors. I want you to have the goods. But I don't care where you go. I love you. We love you. No matter what! Wherever you go, I love you, and we'll be thrilled."

As my dad spoke, the shaking subsided and then stopped. I began to calm down. He continued, "Kenny, I'm so proud of you. You have so far exceeded anything I could possibly have expected from you. You were a fat, clumsy kid. You and your hard work are responsible for how amazingly well you've turned out. We both love you, and we're always behind you.

"Remember, I came from practically nothing. I had to fight for everything I have. I'm thrilled with how you've turned out. I don't give a damn about Harvard or where you go. Do you hear me?"

I heard him. I felt his love. I believed him. My dad then shook my hand and said, "Okay?" I heard what he said, but I couldn't respond. He then shook my hand again and said with much more vigor, "Okay?"

I answered in as positive a manner as possible under the circumstances. "Okay."

My dad leaned over and kissed me on the cheek. Then my mom slid over and held me. I needed both.

After a moment, she said, "Kenny, you've made me so proud to be your mother. You're the best thing I've ever done." She then kissed my other cheek.

As I went back to my room, my dad told me, "Kenny, always remember, we love you!"

Over the next couple of days, I wasn't quite myself. It was as if I were in a daze. There, but not really. Hearing, but not listening. Seeing, but not absorbing. A very weird state.

After that, I wrote the "Superman" poem below, and then life went on as usual. As I expected, I didn't get into Harvard Law School, and I was okay with it. I was happy to be accepted into Cornell's business and law program. I looked forward to having the new experience of living in the idyllic setting of Ithaca, New York.

As time went on, I reflected upon the fact that I had felt a great deal of pressure to succeed, being the only child of two loving and giving parents, both of whom poured their dreams, hopes, and expectations into me. For better or worse.

Another reason why it is so important to make your life choices free of expectations or pressures that are being exerted upon you is because you want to make a decision that is right for you in the long term of your life. You don't want to make a choice that gives you and those you're trying to please the short-term, quick-fix gratification of meeting their expectations and goals for you. Understanding and appreciating all of this, you should also aspire higher and not put these kinds of intense, unhealthy pressures on others to meet your subjective expectations and goals for them.

As we discussed earlier, life-choice-making is like playing chess in that one move or decision can materially impact many other moves, options, and choices down the road. So when making your life choices, always view the big picture of how a particular move or life choice that you make today will affect others down the road.

Be astutely Consequence Cognizant. Therefore, you need to make decisions and choices that are consistent with and reflective of YOUR goals, YOUR dreams, and YOUR highest values, not somebody else's.

In your efforts to fill your *Heart-of-Hearts* with positives, high self-esteem, confidence, and love, you don't want to fill your *Heart-of-Hearts* with bitterness, second-guessing, or regrets because you made decisions based upon someone else's values, expectations, insecurities, and agendas.

SUPERMAN

(The pressures of feeling others' expectations for you)
A superman is always strong,
Fighting evil all day long.
Never feeling any pain,
Always saving Lois Lane.

While others may not have a clue,
He always knows just what to do.
He jumps tall buildings at a whim,
Everyone looks up to him.
Invariably he gets it right,
He obviously is Super-bright.
Always doing more than expected.
Not a single problem is ever detected.

(But in truth, this would-be "Superman")
Fights to hold back every tear,
Represses every hurt and fear.
And would never express how confused he feels.

Not the heroic "Man of Steel."
High expectations can be such a load,
At any point, he may well implode.
He's one step away from his ungluing,
'Cause he doesn't know what the hell he's doing . . .

Except trying to be what his parents expect.
Not someone they will both reject.

He seeks perfection for appearance sake,
This adolescent Super-fake.
But he's not sure how much he can take,
Before his heart and soul just break.

And every night, while he's in bed,
The very same thought runs through his head . . .
I hope one day that I'll be free,
To feel good enough . . . to just be me.
And they'll encourage me to pursue,
The things I truly want to do.
And if I do the best I can,
I won't have to be a "Superman."

—KL

27

PAY GREAT ATTENTION TO THE "HOW"

*Everyone wants to live on top of the
mountain, but all of the happiness and
growth occurs while you're climbing it!*
—ANDY ROONEY

*Your self-esteem in large part depends
on the means you choose to attain your ends.*
—KL

In our society, we often applaud and reward the individual who
succeeds—that is, we laud the person who lands the big account,
the sought-after news interview, the lofty promotion, along with the
individuals who win the Super Bowl, the Tour de France, the Major
League Home Run title, and the like. We are truly an ends-focused
society that pays little or no attention to the means of goal attainment. However, the individual who follows the *PLCP* quite often
takes the road less traveled, and in this instance, we believe that

HOW you conduct your life and your business is as important and, in certain instances, even more important than whether you attain your coveted ends.

We have all heard or seen stories about individuals who have allegedly cheated and violated rules to get ahead. Of course, exponentially more individuals whom we don't know about have compromised themselves and their feelings of self-esteem and self-worth by breaking the rules to secure the victory, grab the gold ring, and bask in the adulation and press clippings. The profound problem with this behavior is that whether or not these individuals' bad behavior comes to light, deep down the perpetrators know the hard and cold truth: that they didn't feel that they had the goods to succeed without cheating, behaving badly, hurting others, and/or acting inappropriately.

Aspire Higher is all about making positive choices that will instill feelings of self-love, high self-esteem, and self-worth into your *Heart-of-Hearts*. So, if you cheat others or the system, hurt, are insensitive, disrespectful, destructive to others, or are divisive and toxic, you can't hide the truth from your *Heart-of-Hearts*, and you will on some level feel bad about how you acted and about yourself. These negative feelings, along with your negativity bias, in turn will lead you to develop and harbor feelings of low self-esteem and a lack of true confidence. In lieu of self-loving, you will experience highly virulent feelings of self-loathing. These pernicious feelings will lead you to make poor life choices in the future, because you won't feel that you're worthy of making good and beneficial choices, and you won't have the authentic confidence that you have the ability to truly elevate the quality of your life.

Conversely, if you are proud of how you act and the person that you are, you develop feelings of high self-esteem and self-worth, which lead to self-love and positive, beneficial, and highly constructive life choices. And, if you can act in a manner that you are proud of and feel good about AND you attain your coveted goals, even more positives will be instilled and embedded into your *Heart-of-Hearts*!

This chapter is in no way meant to be preachy or moralistic; rather, it is purely practical. If you want to feel good about yourself, proud of yourself, and develop the requisite amount of self-love that will lead you to make great life choices for yourself and others, it's crystal clear that the way you act and live your life, your means of goal attainment, and the content of your character count BIG TIME in determining whether you will live the life you dream about and be your best self.

Along with doing the right thing, it's so important to be kind. The other day, I read the following insight: "Just one person saying to me, 'You've made my day!' makes my day!'"[1] You have the awesome power to make such a positive impact on an individual's day and possibly their life by taking the time and making the effort to be kind, caring, and compassionate. Ideally, because your goal is to aspire higher, you will altruistically express your kindness to someone with no thought of any karmic or other payback to you, which, as we've said, is the highest form of behavior. However, as it turns out, your reward for being kind and thoughtful will be huge, as you will instill highly potent feelings of self-esteem and self-worth into your *Heart-of-Hearts* when you show kindness and empathy to and compassion and love for others. Lifting others lifts you, your self-image, your confidence to positively impact others, and your spirits. It's truly powerful stuff! Please remember the adage "There are many times that being kind is more important than being right."[2]

28

THE ENERGY OF OUR SPIRITS AND SOULS LIVE ON AFTER "DEATH"

If you wish to find me, look for
me in my children and theirs.
—GEORGE FEDER,
the father of my friend Bart Feder

Energy cannot be created or destroyed but only converted from one form to another.[1] Put another way, the energy of human beings when they die isn't destroyed, but rather, it is transformed into another form and exists on another plane.

I am of the mind that when people pass, the energy from their souls and spirits lives on. So, when we lose our cherished loved ones, we can be comforted by the idea that not only can they be found in our loving memories of them and in their children, but they are also still very much with us and are watching over us, as they continue to exist and are with us in spirit-energy.

I understand that this is a controversial theory that I'm espousing, but I'd like to share a couple of personal stories on the subject.

My parents, Betty and Jack, and I lived by the beach in Brooklyn, New York, for most of my childhood. One of the main ways that my father and I spent time together and bonded was by going swimming in the ocean a block or so from our home, and in a pool at the local beach club. My dad loved to swim, and throughout my life, he strongly suggested that I keep up my swimming as a means to get great exercise while not taxing or damaging my body as he perceived my playing tennis on hard courts with regularity did. My dad worked and swam until he was nearly ninety-nine years old. He often told me that the reason why his body didn't break down during all those years and why his posture was so excellent was that swimming loosened and massaged his muscles and his body. Put succinctly, he was a huge proponent of me swimming throughout my life to preserve the quality of my physical well-being, my life, and my longevity. I also have the most beautiful, heartfelt, and indelible memories of walking to the ocean in the evenings with my dad when he returned home from a hard day's work. We'd take wonderful, invigorating swims together. Then we'd walk home, talk, smell the magnificent salt air, and view the brilliant sunsets over the ocean. These were some of my most wonderful times, and now they are among my most stirring early teenage memories.

Throughout my adult life, my father would remind me of how beneficial swimming is. He did his best to lead by example by swimming almost every day—especially after he and my mom moved to Los Angeles.

At about ninety-eight years old, my dad started to develop memory challenges, as he'd repeat stories that he had recently shared. As time passed, this behavior became more prevalent. When he turned one hundred, he also suffered from Alzheimer's, although by no means the most severe form of it. When his body started to break down, I spent countless hours with him in the hospital. Every fifteen minutes or so, as if he were on a loop, he would ask me the same question: "Kenny, are you swimming? You know how it's helped me last so long, and it can help you." And each time, I'd respond, "Dad, the pool heater is broken, and no one has been able to fix it. Besides, I want to be here [in the hospital] with you. I'll get it fixed once you're out of here and on the mend." This give-and-take took place throughout each day until he went into a coma a day or so before he passed, when his body just gave out. A few moments before his heart stopped, he woke from his coma and motioned to me in disdain that he didn't want to be hooked up to all of the contraptions that were keeping him alive. He then said his last few words to me: "Kenny, I have no regrets. I've had a great life, and I love you and Betty." He then paused for a moment and smiled sweetly, as he asked me for the last time, "Are you swimming? It's really good for you!" And I for the last time explained that the pool heater was broken, and it was too cold to swim with it not working. My dad passed a moment or two later.

My dad passed on a Thursday afternoon. His funeral was held that Sunday. Much of my time during the intervening days was spent making funeral arrangements. We had a great and loving turnout as we celebrated my father's wonderful life. When everyone left the post-funeral gathering at my home that Sunday afternoon, I was too tired to reflect upon all that had transpired over the past few days and didn't give anything much thought, other than to confirm in my mind that I was going to go to work the next day—just as I believed my dad would have wanted me to and would have done if the roles had been reversed. He never missed work.

I fell asleep early that evening. The next morning, I awoke to a somber, gray, overcast sky. Now that the proverbial music and tumult of my father's passing had abruptly stopped and all was quiet, I was left with the stark, cold reality that I would never see or speak with my loving dad again. As those who have lost cherished loved ones can attest, no feeling is worse. I have always been one to do my best to take a constructive and an optimistic approach to all challenges and setbacks. Why? Because I believe that there is always a creative way to succeed . . . and there is always hope. In this case, there was no way and no hope that I would see, be with, and talk with my dad ever again. The dark finality of it all hit me with a thud and oh so sharply struck my *Heart-of-Hearts*, core of my being, and my soul. My sweet, beloved dad was gone forever!

I did my best to power through showering, shaving, dressing, and having breakfast, feeling the deepest emptiness. I was certainly moving a good deal slower than I normally would have. When I looked outside, the sky was still gray. I thought, *If it were only a bit sunnier . . . if the sky were only bluer, I might feel a bit better*, as sunshine and blue skies always lifted my spirits. Finally, I dragged through my morning prep process and opened the front door.

Interestingly, I looked up and saw a hint of sunshine breaking through the clouds. I felt a bit better. Then something miraculous happened! As I took a step or two into my driveway, a truck pulled up to my home. I immediately thought, *Who am I expecting?* A moment later I concluded that I wasn't expecting anyone. But then I saw the side of the truck and the warmest, most beautiful feeling shot through my being. The side of the truck read "POOL HEATING FIXED." Tears began to stream down my cheeks. I walked up to the man in the truck and asked, "Can I help you?"

He smiled and said, "Yes, I'm here to fix your pool heater." I told him that I hadn't called for anyone to fix my pool heater.

I then asked him what address he was supposed to be going to. We then realized that he was at the wrong home. I asked him his name, and with a warm smile he replied, "Pepe." I then told Pepe that it was the craziest thing, but my pool heater had been broken for months, and the two pool maintenance people who had come to my home to try to fix the problem had been baffled. The pool parts remained strewn in the grass in the backyard. Pepe with great kindness said that he was early for his appointment and would take a look.

A couple of moments later, Pepe reemerged and said with glowing confidence, "I can fix your heater. I'll go to my appointment, and when I'm done, I'll go get the parts I need and be back this afternoon to work on it. You'll be swimming before the end of the day!"

I thanked Pepe profusely as tears once again streamed down my cheeks. I realized that my dad had just communicated with me in a language and in a manner that I would totally understand and appreciate: "Kenny, don't be sad. I lived a great life! I have no regrets. It was my time to go. Go to work. Enjoy your life. I love you and I'm always with you. So NOW, would you get the darn pool heater fixed and start swimming?"

Later that day, Pepe came back and fixed the heater . . . and I swam that afternoon with a fervor and a freedom like no other, knowing that my dad was still with me, just in another energy form, on another plane.

But wait, there's more! In 2018, my mom, Betty, passed away. That was a little over two and a half years ago. For a substantial period of time, I didn't hear anything from her. I had received no clear sign that my mom's spiritual energy was "out there," as I had experienced with my dad a few years earlier. That said, I continued to feel in my *Heart-of-Hearts* that my mom's energy, soul, and spirit were with me, just like my dad's.

Throughout the last few years of my mom's life, she was convinced that our son, Tristan, would make a wonderful architect. She often would watch Tristan play the internet game Minecraft, and she would remark that he had the hands and mind of an architect. She encouraged him in every way she could to pursue architecture. She would often strongly suggest to me that when our family goes to New York City we should go to the 3M Museum, as the architecture exhibits there would inspire him. My mom would repeatedly remind me of this whenever she thought about Tristan. One day, I looked up the 3M Museum, only to find that no such museum existed in New York City. I attributed my mom's mistake to the occasionally faltering memory of a person in their nineties.

Then, on a Sunday afternoon, about a year and a half after my mom had passed, I was walking in Manhattan when I looked up to see the building whose address was 666 Fifth Avenue. Within a second, I realized that this was the building that my mom and I had visited about twenty years earlier, when I was looking for office space in New York City. I vividly remembered that I really liked the office space I saw there, but my mom didn't want me to rent in that building, because she thought that the three sixes in the address would be unlucky. Due to her strong feeling about the address, I chose not to rent in that building. As I recalled our experience there, I smiled. A second later, I happened to look across the street, and there was a museum . . . and in front of it, in big and bold writing was "3M." Incredibly, they were advertising a new architecture exhibit!

At that moment, the very same warm feeling shot through my body that I had experienced years earlier when Pepe, in his POOL HEATING FIXED truck, pulled up to my home after my dad's passing. Once again, I had a parent communicating with me in a language and in the means that I would undeniably understand, recognize, and take note of. It was my mom's way of telling me that she, too, is there and with me.

That evening, in the quiet of my hotel room, I thought about both of the experiences of connecting with my parents. They brought to mind the fact that I had read a compelling book, years earlier, titled *Talking to Heaven: A Medium's Message of Life After Death*, by James Van Praagh, who is a celebrated medium. Van Praagh, in his book, depicts instances where he connected with the spirits of individuals who have passed on.[2] Upon reading *Talking to Heaven*, a year or two after my dad's passing, I was both intrigued and skeptical. As I continued to reflect upon Pepe and the 3M Museum events, I wondered whether Van Praagh was channeling the same energy forces that I had connected with when I received clear messages from my dad and mom. It certainly seemed logical.

Until we ourselves pass, we will never truly know if my perception and interpretation of these events is correct. I, in my *Heart-of-Hearts*, believe that it is. That said, I hope what you can glean and believe from all of this is that the energy, spirit, and soul of those you love who have passed on are still with you, loving you, wanting the very best for you, and watching over you. They are simply now on a different energy plane. I sincerely hope that this belief comforts you, buoys you, and gives you authentic optimism that treasured loved ones are still with you and that you, through your spiritual energy, will one day be reunited with them.

29

IMPORTANT
LIFE LESSONS

We all have moments and days that test us, bring us down, frustrate us, and infuriate us. It's part of the life process. As we have said, you often can't control the events that take place in your life, but you can take ownership of your responses and not allow your negativity bias to exacerbate the situation and send you, your spirit, and your day spiraling downward. One means to do this is to keep things in their proper perspective so you keep your composure, positive attitude, and equilibrium. Along the lines of keeping things on an even keel and on a positive note, I'd like to share a poem that I wrote years ago after I met a man named Dan.

SO YOU THINK THAT
YOUR DAY'S BEEN ROUGH?

As I rushed through the terminal to catch my plane,
Business worries and hassles filled my brain.
And while quickly perusing fax after fax,
I briefly glanced up and stopped dead in my tracks.

All alone he stood, with two bags and a cane,
I watched for some time and alone he remained.
No one assisted this blind young man.
I then quickly walked over, and I met Dan.

He said he'd been standing for twenty minutes or so,
He had a plane to catch, but he didn't know,
How he'd get his ticket or find his gate,
With no one to help him, he feared he'd be late.

Dan's mom had arranged for an airline attendant,
Upon whom Dan would be totally dependent,
To help him navigate through a world he can't see.
As no one showed up, Dan's guide would be me.

I looked at the flight board, as a start,
So we'd know from which gate, Dan's plane would depart.
I realized our time was much more than tight,
To get his ticket; find the gate; and make his flight.
I tried to stay calm and not show my alarm.
We picked up Dan's bags; he grabbed hold of my arm.

As we carefully began to wend our way,
Inside I cried and fervently prayed,
For God to do, all He possibly can,
To make life much better for all of the "Dans."

The rush hour commuters—made us move slow,
Dan relying on someone he couldn't see, didn't know.
When we finally made it to the gate,
For the moment I thought we weren't "too late."

Until the gate attendant waved to me in a flurry,
"Run down to those steps," she said. "Better hurry."
"And if you run to that bus, you can take it."

Then she saw Dan and whispered, "But he'll never make it."
My heavy heart sank down to my knees,
I begged the attendant to help us please:
"Delay the bus, the flight—use all of your power."
As the next flight for Dan, would be in five hours.

But this is a truly sorry tale,
My exhortations were to no avail.
I then went over and broke the news to Dan,
And promised that I'd do all that I can,
To make sure that he would be all right,
And that he'd make the very next flight.

He then realized that his brother Jim,
Would be at the airport waiting for him.
Dan nervously asked, "Please take me to a phone."
But when he called up his brother, nobody was home.

I then brought Dan back to his gate.
I soon had to leave him, or I, too, would be late.
It was then that we learned, that the very next flight,
Would depart from a building, one block to our right.
I then explained to a "rep," the whole tragic state,
That if the attendant had been there,
Dan would not have been late.

The "rep" said, "We'll have someone escort your friend.
And on that, sir, you can depend."
Leaving Dan for my plane, was so very hard.
As I left, I handed him my business card.
I asked him to call me and keep in touch.
He thanked me very, very much.

And as I walked off, to catch my plane,
Few times have I felt deeper pain.
Feeling guilty that I haven't done all I can,
To help others like, my fellow Dan.

As I left to take my flight back home,
There sat Dan—on his own.
For the next few hours, he had but one thing to do:
Wait for the next arm to hold on to.
Until then, in his seat he'd park.
All alone. In the dark.

So, when I think that I've had a "bad day,"
In my mind, Dan's story I replay.
I then invariably come to find,
As to my many blessings—I've been so blind.

I learned a lot on that fateful trip,
Which helps me get a better grip.
As I now realize it would be truly sad,
Should I come to feel, that my day's been bad.

—KL

"ROCKIN' THAT EXTRA CHROMOSOME!"— THE RUBY'S RAINBOW SCHOLARSHIP FUND[1]

Probability is not destiny.

—STEVE PRICE,

from a letter he wrote for his 35th
Harvard University reunion

Just as I was finishing this book, my wonderful wife, Melinda, showed me the most inspiring video of a young man named Jeremy, who has Down syndrome. The video shows Jeremy taking his college courses online due to the pandemic. As you watch this video, entitled "Surf's Up!," which can be found on the *Positive Life Choice Psychology* website, you learn that Jeremy, along with taking his college courses, has a part-time job at a restaurant, is a mentor to a young boy with Down syndrome, has a lovely and loving girlfriend, has many friends, and loves to surf.[2] His wonderful mother, Lisa, says that Jeremy finds surfing "freeing" and "transformative," as the water seems to free the highly positive Jeremy from some of his daily trials and tribulations.

Interestingly, Lisa shared with me that one of the main reasons why she thinks that Jeremy and his development have met and exceeded all expectations is that she set the bar of expectations high for Jeremy. Essentially, this belief in him and his potentials propelled Jeremy to aspire higher and to ultimately shine and thrive. When I asked Lisa what she has learned from her experiences with Jeremy, she offered two insights: First, she and others identify what Jeremy's strengths are and make the most of them; and second, they emphasize his blessings and, with great positivity, work through and support his challenges. Put another way, they have focused with great success on the many things that Jeremy is able to do, not on the limiting Down syndrome label ascribed to him and all that it connotes.

The powerful takeaway here is that your happiness in large part lies in how you choose to look at things. For example, if we attach the highly diminishing term "disabled" to individuals with Down syndrome, our perception and focus are all about what they cannot do. The first three letters of "disabled"—"dis"—are all about discounting them, their capabilities, and the vital role that they can play in our society. I suggest that we instead choose to look at their many abilities to thrive in life, as Jeremy and a plethora of others with Down syndrome are doing everyday. In other words, dismiss the "dis" and celebrate the "able." Similarly, like Lisa and Jeremy, wouldn't it be great if we all consciously choose to focus much more of our time and energies on our blessings, gifts, abilities, and the wonderful people and things in our lives? This positive choice will most certainly elevate us and all those around us.

I believe that everyone can benefit and be inspired by the twenty-one-year-old Jeremy, as he is not only persevering with his Down syndrome challenges but thriving with them. As you can see from the video, Jeremy knows and understands his condition, yet his heart is full of love, serenity, and optimism, as he looks forward to living on his own. His mom says that Jeremy often joyfully tells her and others that "I love my life!" and that "I have a great life!"

Lisa has done a spectacular parenting job, and Jeremy, with great authenticity and a *Heart-of-Hearts* full of love, tells her so, and reinforces this huge compliment with a big, loving hug. Jeremy, in every way, is "rockin' that extra chromosome" that he was born with. He is a genuine, living example of someone who is making the most of the cards that he has been dealt and is busy fulfilling his many potentials. Jeremy is a true inspiration and role model for us all to make the most of our lives and the challenges that we have been handed.

Here's to aspiring higher. Here's to you, Jeremy! You're one of my heroes!

Hearing Jeremy's inspiring story, I thought about my own evolution. Throughout my early life, I was often told what I couldn't do. Besides my mom, and maybe a small handful of other supportive individuals, no one expected me to achieve very much. However, with a few encouraging, key people in my life, I was able to make positive life choices, which led to the development of empowering feelings of confidence and a positive, optimistic mind set. As a result, I have been able to fulfill many of my potentials and have found my voice, callings, and inner happiness. I respectfully suggest that you make one of your preeminent goals to fortify and nourish your life with positives: positive people, positive choices, and a positive and constructive way of viewing and dealing with people and events.

And also, please remember, as Steve Price so wisely observed, probability isn't destiny. Through your positive life choices, you can take control of your destiny and blaze your own wonderful life path!

WISDOM

Wisdom is defined as "the quality of having experience, knowledge, and good judgment; the quality of being wise."[1] For *The PLCP Lifestyle*, wisdom encompasses much more. It involves having the emotional intelligence to deftly navigate personal relationships and interactions, as well as day-to-day life; having the knowledge and instincts to know what behavior is appropriate in a given situation; the ability to know or intuit the appropriate timing to engage or refrain from engaging in certain acts; and the ability to effectively connect and communicate with others, and touch, positively impact, support, and elevate them. So, wisdom is a special and power-packed word, as it enables you to accomplish so many wonderful things and positively impact so many lives.

You want to strive to be an astute and wise decision-maker for three important reasons: First, every wise choice that positively impacts you and others makes you feel good about yourself and what you were able to accomplish. This organically instills positive feelings of high self-esteem and mastery into your *Heart-of-Hearts*, which, as we have discussed, can trigger all sorts of healthy choices and acts in the future. Second, being wise and acting wisely in situations is confidence building, empowering, and self-esteem enhancing—all things that once again fill your *Heart-of-Hearts* with positives. Third, being wise is akin to a sort of superpower, as you can make such a ripple-effect difference in your life, the lives of others, and the world. We all can use wise individuals in our lives.

For so many reasons, strive to become a wise life-choice maker!

BEING WISE

What helps cut problems down to size?
And lets you see through a disguise?
What dictates which response applies?
It's the quality of being wise.
Being clever and being smart,
Don't make you wise, but they're a start.
It's not just thinking with your heart.
Wisdom requires a higher art.
Being wise knows, that if you are to flourish
Your spirit and soul you'll have to nourish.
Because if in life you get ahead,
It won't mean much, if your soul is dead.
As you look back and see time fly,
And you feel empty and wonder why,
Seeing the erosion and the compromise,
And all the times when you weren't wise.
But the wise know that it's a brand-new day,
When you're ready to do and say, that
Instead of settling . . . I'm going to reach for the skies,
By making positive life choices, through being wise.

—KL

PRECIOUS MOMENTS

Just as I was completing this book, I received some alarming news from a longtime friend, "Jennifer," who was stricken with cancer. When I spoke with Jennifer, she said that when she received the diagnosis, she was shocked. She had always been so healthy. She was scared beyond words and paralyzed with fear. Jennifer had three young children and was terrified of leaving them without a mother.

A few days later, Jennifer underwent surgery to remove the malignancy. Fortunately for her, the doctor said that he believes that all of the cancer was removed and that there is a very good chance that she can make a strong and full recovery. Jennifer told me that she could not be more grateful for the positive prognosis. During one of our post-surgery calls, she said that she is truly "euphoric" to be alive and a "new woman"! She then shared that every moment is now a "precious moment," which is the title of one of her favorite jazz songs.[1]

I have always perceived Jennifer as a wise and centered individual, and I'm sure that she valued her wonderful life with her beautiful family before being told about her potential life-changing/life-ending illness, but there's no question that this kind of catastrophic news and event can serve to make even the most evolved individual appreciate their precious moments far more.

A few days after Jennifer shared her story with me, I learned that Steve Price, the brother of my treasured friend and client Dave Price, passed away after battling pancreatic cancer. I would like to share an excerpt from Dave's beautiful and moving eulogy for his beloved brother.

"It would be easy to slide into despair—but as much as I hurt, I am grateful. Doctors, nurses, medical staff, social workers, volunteers, advocates, friends, family, and complete strangers locked arms with Steve and gave us four and a half years that we never expected. Every day was hard fought and won. Every day was precious."

Interestingly, the word "precious" was used by two individuals in connection with two different events, one potentially catastrophic (Jennifer learning that she had substantial brain cancer) and the other devastating (Steve passing away from pancreatic cancer). There is a great life lesson here. Of course, at any time in our lives, whenever the epiphany comes, it's great and incredibly beneficial to make the positive life choice to highly value every precious moment that we're blessed to enjoy, but this insight leads to a game-changing question: Why do we have to wait for a bad, unfortunate, or catastrophic event to occur that breaks up our status quo and/or life-spirit malaise, before we decide to up our game and begin to truly and with great passion and appreciation treasure our precious moments? In other words, why must we so oftentimes be reactive, when we can be so positively proactive, by making the very most of our lives, our well-being, and our precious moments *before* something bad happens to us or to someone or something we love?

We are a reactive, quick-fix society. We don't generally focus on issues that need fixing or remedying until something bad happens, is egregious, or intolerable. Then we turn our attention to the problem for the moment, until something else quickly takes our attention-impaired focus away to the next issue, challenge, or subject. To live your highest and best life, starting today, strive to be proactive, wise, and in the moment (hineni) by treasuring, appreciating, and being grateful for all of your precious moments as they happen—whether they be wonderful or challenging—while you're here on earth. This way, when you look back on your day, your year, and your life and how well and thoroughly you lived it, you'll feel like you made the most of it and totally self-actualized. How truly great, constructive, and wise would that be?

Referring back to Dave's eulogy, after reading a brilliant and incredibly touching letter that Steve wrote for his thirty-fifth college reunion, Dave shared this beautiful insight: "My brother's own words summarize his humanity better than I ever could. 'Love and be loved, care and be cared for, be brave, and be positive. Make your time worth it.'"

As someone who seeks to aspire higher, starting today, do your very best to treat every day, event, person, relationship, gift, challenge, and life choice as precious. By doing this, you are doing everything in your power to elevate the quality of your life, the lives of others, and the world.

CARPE DIEM

Gather ye Rosebuds while ye may,
Old Time is still a-flying:
And this same flower that smiles today,
Tomorrow will be dying.

—From "To the Virgins, to Make
Much of Time" by Robert Herrick

Carpe diem is Latin for "seize the day" or "seize the moment." For *The PLCP Lifestyle*, carpe diem is brimming with energy and emotion. It means that while you're alive, you have the ability to seize opportunities to make positive, constructive, and loving choices that raise the quality of your life and those of others.

Pro tennis legend and pioneer Billie Jean King said regarding the process of competing: "Pressure is a privilege." The same thing can be said about life-choice-making. The golden opportunities that require you to make choices that will change your life and those of others in the most positive and beneficial ways are a privilege to seize joyfully. Please remember, starting today, you can change the course of your life for the so much better by the choices that you make!

Carpe diem also signifies our ability to seize the opportunity to elevate others, be a cohesive and collaborative force, help someone, share a word of kindness, and make this world a better, more peaceful, and love-filled place.

Carpe diem is all about being opportunistic and seizing memorable moments, like savoring a beautiful sunset or sunrise; hugging or kissing someone you love; smelling fresh-cut grass, the salty ocean breeze, or a rose or gardenia; watching your child playing soccer, acting in a school play, playing an instrument; or having your dog or cat on your lap, unconditionally loving you as you love and treasure them. You can default to a negativity bias mode, or you can proactively seize the beauty in life and its many miracles . . . so many of which are free for the viewing and enjoying. Put yourself in positions to have experiences that will make your *Heart-of-Hearts* well up with joy, appreciation, gratitude, and the love of being alive! Seize those soul-nourishing moments and fill your *Heart-of-Hearts* with love. Consciously choose to be positive and happy. Carpe diem!

The following is a poem I wrote about the joyful, optimistic, proactive spirit of carpe diem.

CARPE DIEM

Carpe diem—seize the day!
Live your life in a vital way.
Learning from experiences, as they go by,
Proactively dealing with stimuli.

Carpe diem—seize the day!
It's something that feels so good to say!
Devour life, make it great,
Make things happen, don't be a victim of fate.

Carpe diem—seize the day!
Don't stand there—with feet of clay.
Be prepared—don't get caught short.
Battles are won before they are fought.

Carpe diem—even when times are rough!
I'll test my mettle—see if I have the stuff.
And if I don't, I won't wallow in sorrow,
I'll just learn from mistakes and be better tomorrow.

Carpe diem—with all your might!
Be a constant source of light.
And do all you can, in hopes that you might
Lift all those you touch, to greater heights.

Carpe diem—seize the day!
But don't do it in a selfish way.
Along with coveting opportunism,
Be a shining example of altruism.

And when I seize my final day,
From the core of my being, I will pray.
That when there's a final "history,"
I can say, "I'm proud of me."

—KL

PUTTING ALTRUISTIC LOVE INTO ACTION

*If we could change ourselves, the
tendencies in the world would also
change. As a man changes his own
nature, so does the attitude of the world
change toward him. This is the divine
mystery supreme. A wonderful thing it
is and the source of our happiness.*

—MAHATMA GANDHI

These words of Gandhi have been paraphrased over the years to become the popular saying "Be the change you want to see in the world." And although Gandhi's original words may have held deeper meaning, this well-known interpretation is also true. Once you've filled your *Heart-of-Hearts* with empowering, positive, highly motivating feelings, discovered how to make cognitively clear choices that reflect your highest self, established what your highest values and goals are, and learned to effectively use the *Positive Life*

Choice Psychology Philosophies, you can aspire even higher to spread your love and positivity to others. When you reach this height of Altruistic Love, you can begin to be the positive change in the world that you want to see, in small or large ways.

TAKING STEPS TO CHANGE THE WORLD

Whether your new sense of well-being and full *Hearts-of-Hearts* lead you to begin the ripple of positive change by doing small but meaningful things for those around you or by spreading positivity and love on a grander scale, you can take active steps to change the world. You don't have to be rich or famous to make a difference. Anyone can spread love, beginning with some loving baby steps.

You can start small and fill up your *Heart-of-Hearts* even more by doing random acts of kindness such as helping your elderly neighbor by mowing his yard, for instance. Perhaps offer to babysit a single mom's children for an afternoon while she runs errands. Or spread your reach even farther and use your professional talents to start a program to help those who can benefit from your expertise.

If you have the time, you can volunteer in your community, and if you have children, involve them as well so they can learn altruistic behavior from a young age and carry those actions and beautiful, empowering feelings with them into adulthood. What a highly beneficial, lifelong foundation this would be for them!

If you have the financial means, you can donate to your favorite charities, whether in your community or globally. Or simply be kind to those you encounter, sharing a smile and an encouraging or compassionate word. You can also consider other simple ways to pay your blessings forward.

Obviously, these acts help others, but research shows that if you engage in altruistic behaviors, you will also benefit. For example, several studies show that volunteerism is positively correlated with self-reported happiness, health, well-being,[1] and longevity.[2] So not only will you be sharing the love that fills your *Heart-of-Hearts* to help others, but you will also be benefiting yourself! It's a huge, soul-enriching win-win!

BE PROACTIVE WITH CHANGE

Earlier in our journey together, in the section "Precious Moments," we discussed how you don't have to wait until your world is rocked by a bad or an unfortunate event to begin to treat every moment as precious. Our goal is that *before* we suffer a setback that jars us, we want to make the most of every moment in our lives. In other words, let's be positively proactive, not reactive in how we value our time on earth.

We so often learn about a person who experiences a tragedy in their life—such as someone they love contracting or dying from an illness or disease—and that person, whether a parent, child, spouse, or friend, then makes a commitment to be integrally involved with raising money and/or finding a cure for that illness or disease. The individuals who take these kinds of highly admirable cause-and-effect actions are why many wonderful cures have been found and changes have occurred. That said, aspiring higher also calls for you to *proactively* help to find the cure, solve the problem, or better the untenable situation through your volunteerism or other means *before* you or someone close to you is stricken, hurt, or aggrieved. In this way, you can be assured of having a positive impact on our world by being of service to others regardless of your personal experiences.

ANYONE CAN BE THE CHANGE

No matter your means or status in life, you can make a meaningful and highly impactful difference. For example, when your *Heart-of-Hearts* is full and you focus on positive emotions, you can also focus your mindset on how you can share this love with others. Be creative. Think about all of the amazing people—the often-unsung heroes—who work behind the scenes making enormous impacts in people's lives each day. The woman who volunteers at the homeless shelter, reading bedtime stories to the kids; someone who sings to or chats with the elderly; the lawyer who does pro bono work in the community; the young adult who organizes a food drive; or the person who stands with those who are marginalized and fights for their rights.

You can even think smaller and offer to carry someone's groceries for them, pay for the coffee of the person behind you in the drive-thru at Starbucks, and smile and say please and thank you throughout your day. Even these little acts can spread your *Heart-of-Hearts* love and cause a domino effect, changing the world for the so much better.

One Saturday, when my family and I were standing in line to get our COVID-19 vaccines, many individuals were accompanied by their friends and family. As it was a beautiful morning, people were in a chatty mood. But I noticed a young Black man, probably no more than eighteen years old, who was standing in line alone. Everyone was talking around him, but no one was including him in the conversation, which really bothered me. I purposely struck up a conversation with this young man and was able to weave everyone around us into it. Soon he, along with everyone else, was chatting away. A few moments after we all got our shots, the newly formed group all said a warm goodbye to the young man as he left the complex. I believe that this seemingly small incident of purposeful inclusion made a positive difference in all of our lives that day, and who knows what the ripple effect of that interaction will be on the participants? It makes me feel happy and fulfilled every time I envision it.

FINDING YOUR OWN RAINBOW

One of the great gifts of the internet is that it gives us access to a wealth of information about worthy charities, causes, and foundations, which you can research and potentially join. Also, I've witnessed time and time again that a particle in motion attracts other particles in motion, which in this instance calls for you to talk with friends and individuals whom you know and respect about charities, passion projects, and missions they are involved in. Who knows, maybe one or more of those causes might resonate with you and inspire you to join.

For example, my wife, Melinda, who has the most beautiful voice, has been collaborating with legendary music producer Michael Lloyd to record some classic songs. Most recently, Melinda and Michael decided to record a video of Melinda singing "Over the Rainbow." The single's cover art features Dorothy's ruby slippers, just like the ones in *The Wizard of Oz*. One thing led to another, and Melinda learned about the incredible organization Ruby's Rainbow, which we discussed earlier, that grants college scholarships to young adults with Down syndrome. The mission of Ruby's Rainbow struck a deep inner chord with Melinda, especially because our daughter, Mary, aspires to be a teacher or counselor for children with Down syndrome upon college graduation. Melinda is now joyfully committed long term to helping Ruby's Rainbow achieve their inspirational goals, along with the other charity that she encountered through her music, No Kid Hungry. I literally see

Melinda and her soul light up by the new, enriching meaning and higher purpose that she has found by being of service through these organizations. What amazing blessings for everyone involved!

All this to say that if you're active/proactive, attentive, and excited to learn about and be involved with great charities and causes that will positively change and impact our world, you can do it at any level and in any way that you want to or are able. Be a wellspring of Altruistic Love, and realize and embrace the positive impact that you can have on our world. When you are kind to and serve others, and authentically care about those around you, whether you know them or not, your own life and the world will be truly elevated.

A FEW FINAL THOUGHTS

As you have gleaned, the keys to elevating your life, the lives of others, and the world are:

- To fill your *Heart-of-Hearts* with highly positive and empowering feelings of high self-esteem, self-worth, accomplishment, self-confidence, and the like, which are the direct result of aspiring higher and making choices that you are genuinely proud of and feel good about. These feelings transform in your *Heart-of-Hearts* into healthy, extremely potent feelings of self-love, which in turn motivate you to make highly beneficial life choices for yourself, your life, and your well-being. When these feelings in your *Heart-of-Hearts* are strong and/or plentiful enough, with an open, giving, and loving *Heart-of-Hearts*, you will enthusiastically want to help and support others by sharing your love with them. At some point in this process, your self-love and your love for others are transformed in your *Heart-of-Hearts* into the highest love, Altruistic Love. This transformation occurs when you unconditionally make choices and act simply to help, benefit, and lift others because it is the right, respectful, compassionate, loving thing to do. One of your highest aspirations should be to consistently and joyfully practice Altruistic Love.

- To care about, support, and have concern and love for others, while expecting no payback whatsoever. The beautiful, soul-nourishing rewards you receive in the end cannot be more valuable. You continue to fill your *Heart-of-Hearts* with hugely powerful feelings of happiness and pride for elevating the lives and spirits of others, and by aspiring highest, you get to be your best self and live your best life. What humongous, enriching gifts!

- To dissipate or negate the strength and deleterious effects of your potentially toxic emotions so you are able to make cognitively clear life choices that reflect your gold and your truth—which will lead you to be your highest and best self. Successfully implementing this process fills your *Heart-of-Hearts* with the positive feelings that will propel you to want to make more positive life choices for yourself and others in the future.

- To identify your gold and your truth, thereby clearly etching in your mind your highest aspirations so you can be focused and disciplined when making life choices that reflect these aspirations. Effectively performing this process also fills your *Heart-of-Hearts* with empowering, positive feelings of mastery, accomplishment, and confidence.

- To embrace and act consistently with the *PLCP Philosophies, Aspirations, and Ideals* that will organically fill your *Heart-of-Hearts* with self-love and at some point the highest of all loves, Altruistic Love.

- To put your Altruistic Love into action by finding ways to share the love and kindness in your *Heart-of-Hearts* with others. You will then brighten their day, lighten their load, support them, and be their light, anchor, strength, and reliable, trustworthy friend.

As you can see, the key to self-actualizing, being your best self, and living your highest life is to fill your *Heart-of-Hearts* with love through your constructive and enhancing life choices. The exceedingly potent, empowering feelings that are generated by these positive choices will organically catalyze you to do great things for your life and well-being, as well as for the lives and well-being of others.

We are at the end of our journey for now. I hope that it has inspired and motivated you to aspire higher and elevate the quality of your life as well as the lives of others. I know you can give your life great meaning and purpose, fulfill your greatest potential, and enjoy your best life by consistently making positive life choices and following *The Positive Life Choice Psychology Lifestyle*. I also believe that making choices that enhance and are highly beneficial to others will make your life much more meaningful and fulfilling . . . because, as we touched on earlier, "Your song sounds better when we sing it together."

I'd like to close by quoting my treasured friend and longtime client Lester Holt, who ends the *Nightly News* each evening with the following beautiful message: "Please take care of yourself . . . and each other." Along with this beautiful thought, I would respectfully add, "Please love yourself . . . and each other."

Can you imagine how much better our neighborhoods, country, and world would be if everybody heeded the profound messages embodied in those two simple sentences? It would be truly game and world changing.

May you aspire higher so that your *Heart-of-Hearts* is filled with love, happiness, appreciation, and peace!

ACKNOWLEDGMENTS

I would like to acknowledge the wonderful support I always receive from my loving family and adorable doggies, Clara, Bert, and Peanut, as well as from our guinea pig, Weegee. You all make my *Heart-of-Hearts* sing, and each and every day you radiantly light up my life. I so love you all, forever and always.

I acknowledge my incredible parents, Betty and Jack. You have always loved me unconditionally and completely and have been there for me and given me the rock-solid emotional foundation to enable and empower me to live many of my dreams. From you, Mom, I have developed a deep love of psychology and the study of people. You obviously have made a huge contribution to this book and to *The Positive Life Choice Psychology Lifestyle*. Dad, I have learned much of what I know about business, Career Choreography, and deftly navigating relationships from you. Thank you both so much. I'm eternally grateful, and I love you endlessly and always.

I acknowledge the love and support of my extended family: my grandparents, uncles, aunts, cousins, nieces, nephews, the Berman family, the ever-growing Myers family, the Hartley family, the Cammarata family, the Havens family, the Scheer family, our fantastic Ken Lindner & Associates, Inc., clients who have entrusted us with choreographing their precious careers and from whom I've learned so much, and to my KLA family, who have always been there with and for me.

I thank Don Browne for always being so willing to share his abundant wisdom and insights with me. I have learned so much from you, my treasured friend, collaborator, and mentor. You are a true blessing in my life!

I thank Randy Myers for sharing his sage and invaluable insights on the Bible and agape love with me.

I thank Dr. Douglas Krech for teaching me about the exciting field of epigenetics and for always inspiring me to be a scientist, hungry to learn more about the "whys" and the "hows" of life, health, and science.

I thank Dave Price for sharing his beautiful eulogy for his wonderful brother, Steve, with us.

I thank Diane Macedo for giving me the great inspiration to come up with the phrase "Aspire Higher."

I thank Bart Feder for allowing me to print his father, George's, touching headstone message in this book.

I acknowledge the support and love of all of my dear friends. I so treasure and appreciate you all.

I thank all of the individuals who were kind enough to take their valuable time to write a book endorsement. I'm deeply grateful!

I acknowledge some special individuals, without whose help and support this book never would have been written: my terrific executive assistant Shari Freis—only the most superlative adjectives can describe Shari and her stellar work; my wonderful typist and advisor, Edward Miller; Mel Berger—whom I cannot appreciate and respect more; and Marty Singer, whose sage insights and counsel are always invaluable.

I acknowledge the top-drawer individuals at or associated with Greenleaf Publishing who exceed expectations every day and who are amazing in every way: Justin Branch, Jen Glynn, Erin Brown, Ava Coibion, Corrin Foster, Steven Elizalde, Chase Quarterman, Pam Nordberg, and the other wonderful Greenleaf team members. Thank you for always seeing the best in my work and for having the ability and commitment to bring out the best in me and my writing.

I acknowledge the wonderful work and invaluable insights and creativity of the individuals at Total Assault.

Finally, I sincerely thank you, the reader. I hope that you have substantially benefited from reading *Aspire Higher* and learning about *The Positive Life Choice Psychology Lifestyle*. I wish you the best in all of your future endeavors.

To everyone, I hope that you find and enjoy deep and lasting love, and bestow your love on all those whose lives you touch.

APPENDIX

YOUR *GOLD LISTS*

Your *Gold List* comprises what you most dearly want and value in and for your life, as well as what you absolutely don't want in your life, what you abhor, detest, and the like. You can compile two *Gold Lists*: one for all the things you aspire to have or accomplish and one for all the things you do not want or want to get out of your life, which we can call your *ASPIRATIONAL GOLD LIST* and your *TOXIC GOLD LIST*, respectively. You can download all of the following *Lists* at positivelifechoicepsychology.com.

Let's start with an example of an *Aspirational Gold List*. These are the people, things, and events that you dearly want in and for your life, ones that will make your heart sing:

- I want to find deep, lasting love.

- I want to be healthy and enjoy a long, vital, healthy life so that I can be around for my children's weddings and to enjoy my grandchildren.

- I want to be a positive role model for my children.

- I want to spend more time with my children.

- I want to put and keep positive people in my life.

- I want my life to have purpose and meaning.

- I want to lose weight, be thin, and feel better about the way I look. This is important for me, because I want to feel more confident.

- I want to do my part to make this world a better and more peaceful place.

- I want to one day own my own chain of department stores.

- I want to be a partner in my firm.

- I want to stop smoking.

- I want to be in a job that makes me excited to go to work each day.

- I want to spend more time and have a better relationship with my mother/father as he/she won't be around forever.

- I want to streamline and simplify my life.

- I want a better work/life balance, as my life is just passing me by, and my parents won't be here forever and my children won't be living at home much longer.

- I want to spend more quiet time learning about who I am and what I truly want in my life.

Now it's time for you to fill out your *Aspirational Gold List*. Please remember to take your time and be open and truthful.

1. _____
   _____

2. _____
   _____

3. _____
   _____

4. _____
   _____

5. _____
   _____

6. _____
   _____

7. _____
   _____

8. _____
   _____

9. _____
   _____

10. _____
    _____

11. _____

_____

12. _____

_____

13. _____

_____

Okay, now it's time to compile your *Toxic Gold List,* keeping in mind that's it's just as important in making your life choices to know what and who you don't want in your life. Once again, please be scrupulously honest when you make your entries below.

Let me share some examples of things that others have identified that they want out of their life.

- I don't want to have toxic people in my life who bring me down and aren't supportive.

- I don't want to work with or for people who are demeaning and hurtful to me.

- I don't want to watch violent shows or films or listen to misogynistic or hateful music.

- I want to get rid of the clutter in my life, in my head, and in my home.

- I want to get rid of the negativity in my life.

- I don't want to eat fried foods or anything that will raise my cholesterol or clog my arteries.

- I want to stop spending my salary as soon as I receive it; it's time to start saving.

- No more smoking!

- I don't want to settle or compromise regarding the things that are important to me. I deserve better.

- I need to find a new doctor, as I don't want to feel that I'm the last priority on his/her list.

- I must stop drinking too much and drinking and driving.

- No more temper tantrums and letting my uncontrolled temper and anger harm or ruin my relationships.

It's now time for you to fill out your *Toxic Gold List* with the things, people, and events that you want out of your life and those you won't let damage you and/or lower the quality of your life. Once again, please take all the time that you need to make a complete and honest *List*.

1. _____

   _____

2. _____

   _____

3. _____

   _____

4. _____

   _____

5. _____

   _____

6. _____

_____

7. _____

_____

8. _____

_____

9. _____

_____

10. _____

_____

11. _____

_____

12. _____

_____

13. _____

_____

YOUR *TRUTH LIST*

Your next step is to compile your *TRUTH LIST*, which should be composed of the person whom you would ideally like to be, which can include listing the attributes of others that you would like to emulate and incorporate into your behavioral repertoire.

Below are some examples of entries that others have made on their *Truth List*:

- I want to be someone I can be proud of.

- I want to be the change and example that I want to see in the world.

- I want to be a person of God.

- I want to be a father/mother that our children can look up to and be proud of.

- When I die, I want to look back at my life and say that I made a positive difference.

- I want to be the radiant light in the lives of the people I know or impact.

- I want to be a solutionary.

- I want to practice unconditional love, compassion, and generosity.

- I want to put myself in other people's shoes when I make my life choices.

- I want to continue to grow and evolve.

- I want to be truthful.

- I want to have the courage to back up my convictions and beliefs.

- I want to live a life of service to others.

Now it's time to make your own *Truth List*. As you do, please take the time to dig deep down into your *Heart-of-Hearts* and uncover your highest aspirations regarding the person whom you ideally want to be. Once again, in compiling this *List*, be stone-cold honest, as this is your unvarnished, nondefensive truth.

1. _____
   _____

2. _____
   _____

3. _____
   _____

4. _____
   _____

5. _____
   _____

6. _____
   _____

7. _____
   _____

8. _____
   _____

9. _____
   _____

10. _____
_____

11. _____
_____

12. _____
_____

13. _____
_____

After compiling these *Lists*, please read over and absorb them, as they are your personal answers to important and revealing questions. Once you have done this, your goal is to make life choices that reflect and are consistent with your gold and your truth. Also, as time goes on, your gold and truth—which are your PETS—may change as you learn, grow, evolve, and reevaluate what you most want in your life. So from time to time please review these *Lists* to make sure that your entries accurately reflect your most up-to-date valuations. If you need to add new pieces of gold or truth or need to reorder them, please download a new *List* at positivelifechoicepsychology.com.

YOUR "RAINBOW" OR *ALTRUISTIC LOVE EXPRESSION LIST*

Your *Altruistic Love Expression List* is just that—it is composed of the charities, service organizations, activities, passion projects, etc., to meaningfully and purposefully express your Altruistic Love to and for others. This is meant to be a purely personal *List* that reflects what truly touches you, moves you, and calls you to action.

As we discussed earlier, my wife, Melinda, through a serendipitous turn of events learned about two noble charitable organizations, Ruby's Rainbow and No Kid Hungry. The goals of these two charities touched and moved her to such a great degree that I believe that she will be committed to helping them for many years to come.

After taking as much time as you need and doing as much research as you deem necessary, make your personal *Altruistic Love Expression List* below. Remember, these are organizations that you can join and/or contribute to; or you can form your own organization or create and embark on your own personal mission to be of service to others.

Whatever you choose to do and however you choose to be involved, you will be adding oh-so-necessary love, kindness, and caring to our world. As you contemplate your *List* and fill it out, be excited about aspiring higher by finding or adding soul-fulfilling meaning and purpose in and to your life.

When you are ready, please fill out your *List*.

1. _____

   _____

2. _____

   _____

3. _____

   _____

4. _____

   _____

5. _____

   _____

6. _____
   _____

7. _____
   _____

8. _____
   _____

9. _____
   _____

10. _____
    _____

11. _____
    _____

12. _____
    _____

13. _____
    _____

YOUR PERSONAL "ASPIRE HIGHER" PHILOSOPHIES

In Part 4 of this book, I share *The PLCP Lifestyle Philosophies, Ideals*, and *Words* that hopefully resonate with, move, and inspire you. If you would like to think about, identify, and memorialize your own personal philosophies, ideals, and words that move you to aspire higher, please do so below. Experience has taught me that taking the time to search your soul and learn what most inspires you is both cathartic and empowering. I hope that you enjoy the same experience!

_____

_____

_____

_____

_____

_____

_____

_____

_____

_____

_____

_____

_____

_____

_____

_____

_____

_____

_____

Thank you so much for filling out these *Lists*, and may all of your future life choices be highly positive ones!

NOTES

AUTHOR'S NOTE

1. Former US Senator Alan Simpson, speaking at former US President George H. W. Bush's memorial service, 2018.

CHAPTER 1

1. Kendra Cherry, "What Is the Negativity Bias?," verywellmind.com, updated April 29, 2020, https://www.verywellmind.com/negative-bias-4589618.

2. Catherine Moore, "What Is the Negativity Bias and How Can It Be Overcome?," PositivePsychology.com, updated April 26, 2021, https://positivepsychology.com/3-steps-negativity-bias/.

3. Moore, "Negativity Bias."

4. Cherry, "Negativity Bias."

5. Cherry, "Negativity Bias."

6. Cherry, "Negativity Bias."

CHAPTER 4

1. Cherry, "Negativity Bias."

2. I use the word "relatively" because the child is endowed with the genetic scripting of their ancestors.

CHAPTER 8

1. Dr. M. Scott Peck, *The Road Less Traveled* (New York: Touchstone, 1978).

2. Dr. Stephen Covey, *7 Habits of Highly Effective People* (New York: Fireside, 1978).

CHAPTER 9

1. As heard on Colin Cowherd's ESPN radio show.

CHAPTER 10

1. As heard on Colin Cowherd's ESPN radio show.

CHAPTER 12

1. Rudyard Kipling, "If—," Kipling Society.org, accessed May 3, 2021, http://www.kiplingsociety.co.uk/poems_if.htm.

CHAPTER 14

1. Kristen Weir, "Feel Like a Fraud," *gradPSYCH* Magazine, 2013, American Psychological Association, https://www.apa.org/gradpsych/2013/11/fraud.

CHAPTER 16

1. Novak Djokovic, interview by Steve Weissman, Tennis Channel, June 5, 2021.

CHAPTER 18

1. Isabelle Marsh, MSW, "What Does 'Namaste' Actually Mean?," MindBodyGreen.com, updated January 6, 2020, https://www.mindbodygreen.com/0-29229/what-does-namaste-actually-mean.html.

CHAPTER 20

1. Zoe Weil, MA, MTS, "Being a Solutionary," *Psychology Today*, March 14, 2019, https://www.psychologytoday.com/us/blog/becoming-solutionary/201903/becoming-solutionary.

2. Urban Dictionary, "Solutionary," May 15, 2015, https://www.urbandictionary.com/define.php?term=Solutionary.

CHAPTER 21

1. Jessica Tholmer, "Agape Love: Meaning, Origin, and Examples," The Date Mix, March 13, 2019, https://www.zoosk.com/date-mix/love/agape-love/.

2. Tholmer, "Agape Love."

CHAPTER 22

1. A similar quote attributed to Bil Keane, *Family Circus*, August 31, 1994, https://yesterdaytomorrowtodaypresent.blogspot.com/.

2. Cherry, "Negativity Bias."

3. Cherry, "Negativity Bias."

CHAPTER 23

1. Dr. Harold Kushner, *Nine Essential Things I've Learned About Life* (New York: Random House, 2015).

2. Author unknown.

CHAPTER 24

1. I attribute my knowledge of epigenetics to my conversation with Dr. Douglas Krech. There is an unpublished "epigenetics" paper (May 21, 2014) with Dr. Krech and me.

2. Author conversation with Don Browne, former executive vice president of NBC News, former president of Telemundo, and current member of the Broadcasting Hall of Fame, February 13, 2021.

3. Author conversation with Dr. Douglas Krech.

4. Author conversation with Dr. Douglas Krech.

CHAPTER 25

1. "Shalom," The Spiritual Life, accessed May 4, 2021, https://slife.org/shalom/.

CHAPTER 27

1. Quote attributed to Andy Rooney.

2. Quote attributed to F. Scott Fitzgerald.

CHAPTER 28

1. Anne Marie Helminstine, PhD, "The Law of Conservation of Energy Defined," Thought Co., updated January 9, 2020, https://www.thoughtco.com/law-of-conservation-of-energy-605849.

2. James van Praagh, *Talking to Heaven: A Medium's Message of Life after Death* (New York: Penguin, 1999).

CHAPTER 29

1. This saying was originated by Liz Plachta, founder of the Ruby's Rainbow Scholarship Fund, https://rubysrainbow.org/about/.

2. Lisa Fraser (Jeremy's mother) is the head of the Orange County Down Syndrome Foundation. She gave me the information on her son, Jeremy. "Surf's Up" video was originated by the Ruby's Rainbow Scholarship Foundation and was produced and shot by Beyond Measure Media, www.positivelifechoicepsychology.com.

CHAPTER 30

1. "Wisdom," *Oxford Dictionary*, accessed May 4, 2021.

CHAPTER 31

1. Since I heard Jennifer's story, every time I'm irked or thrown off by something or someone, and I might spiral down to a negative place, I think, *precious moments*, and I immediately get back on a positive, constructive course. I do this with the aspiration of not tarnishing, diminishing, or negating what's left of any of my life's precious moments.

CHAPTER 33

1. Wilson J. Musick, MA, "Volunteering and Depression: The Role of Psychological and Social Resources in Different Age Groups," *Social Science & Medicine* 56, no. 2 (2003): 259–269.

2. SG Post, "Altruism, Happiness, and Health: It's Good to Be Good," *International Journal of Behavioral Medicine* 12, no. 2 (2005): 66–77.

ABOUT THE AUTHOR

KEN LINDNER is the founder of *Positive Life Choice Psychology* and *The Positive Life Choice Psychology Lifestyle*. Ken's calling is to envision "what can be" in people, and to equip, enable, and empower ("E3") them to turn their great potential into a highly positive, fulfilling, and productive reality. He graduated from Harvard University magna cum laude, from Cornell Law School, from Brooklyn Polytechnic Preparatory Country Day School (Brooklyn Poly Prep), and from the Brooklyn Ethical Culture School.

In addition to *Aspire Higher*, Ken is the author of five other books: *Career Choreography™: Your Step-by-Step Guide to Finding the Right Job and Achieving Huge Success and Happiness,* in which he shares steps, strategies, and insights regarding how to identify and secure a job or position that's the right fit for you and in which you can shine; *Your Killer Emotions: The 7 Steps to Mastering the Toxic Emotions, Urges, and Impulses that Sabotage You*, in which he presents to readers a plan of action to master their emotions and break their destructive behavioral patterns and bad habits; *Crunch Time: 8 Steps to Making the Right Life Decisions at the Right Times*, which gives readers tried and true emotionally intelligent life strategies that can enable them to fulfill their greatest potentials; and Editions

1 and 2 of *Broadcasting Realities*, which equip broadcast journalists and aspiring broadcast journalists with the essential information they need to make constructive career decisions.

At the heart of all of these books is that your life choices are precious, and if made wisely and strategically, they can change your life in the most wonderful and beneficial ways.

Ken is married to Melinda, and they are blessed to have twins, Mary and Tristan. They also have three adorable dogs, Bert, Clara, and Peanut. The Lindners live in Southern California.